ST. ALBANS TO BEDFORD
INCLUDING THE
HEMEL HEMPSTEAD BRANCH

Geoff Goslin
Series editor Vic Mitchell

MP Middleton Press

Cover Photograph : Standard Class 4MT 4-6-0 No.75042, allocated to Bedford MPD, arrives at Flitwick station with an up stopping train in the late 1950s, before the term commuter was used in this country. (J. Osgood)

First published June 2003

ISBN 1 904474 08X

© Middleton Press

Cover design Deborah Esher

Published by
   Middleton Press
   Easebourne Lane
   Midhurst, West Sussex
   GU29 9AZ
Tel: 01730 813169
Fax: 01730 812601

Layout and typesetting London Railway Record

Printed & bound by Biddles Ltd.
   Guildford and King's Lynn

INDEX

Ampthill	77-82	Heath Park Halt	25
Beaumont's Halt	21	Hemel Hempsted	23-24
Bedford	96-120	Leagrave	50-54
Chiltern Green	29-31	Luton	36-49
Flitwick	68-76	Luton Airport Parkway	32-35
Godwin's Halt	22	Redbourn	20
Harlington	60-67	Roundwood Halt	19
Harpenden	10-18	St. Albans	1-8

ACKNOWLEDGEMENTS

I would like to thank all the photographers whose views appear in this album, together with Dr. John Butcher for kindly supplying illustrations of tickets from his collection.

GEOGRAPHICAL SETTING

The line takes an undulating course across the northern extension of the Chalk of the Chiltern Hills. From Leagrave it descends across Upper Greensand, Gault Clay and Lower Greensand to reach the Ouse Valley.

From Ampthill the track traverses Oxford Clay mostly, this giving rise to the numerous brickworks of the Bedford area.

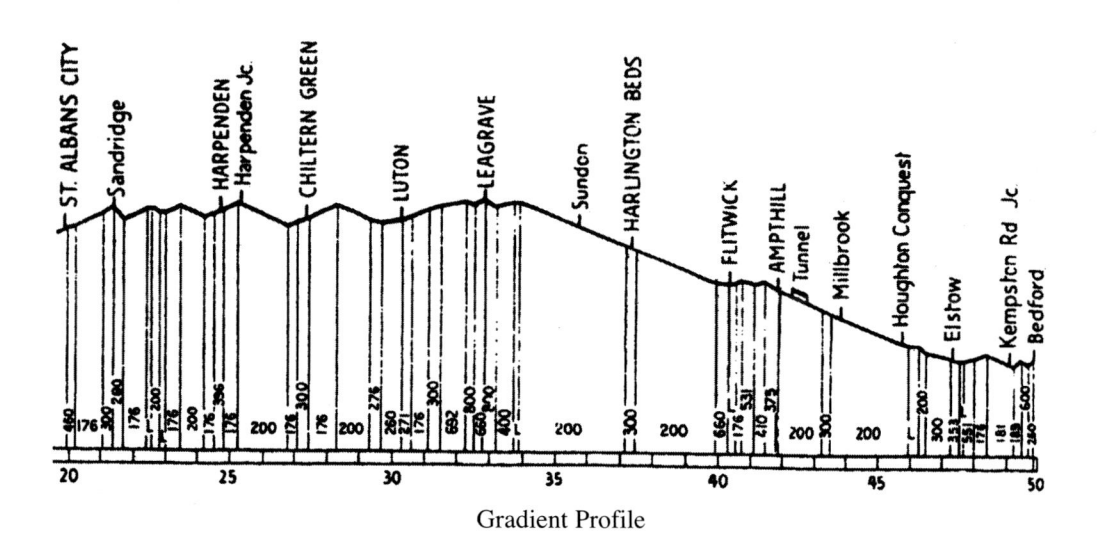

Gradient Profile

IV

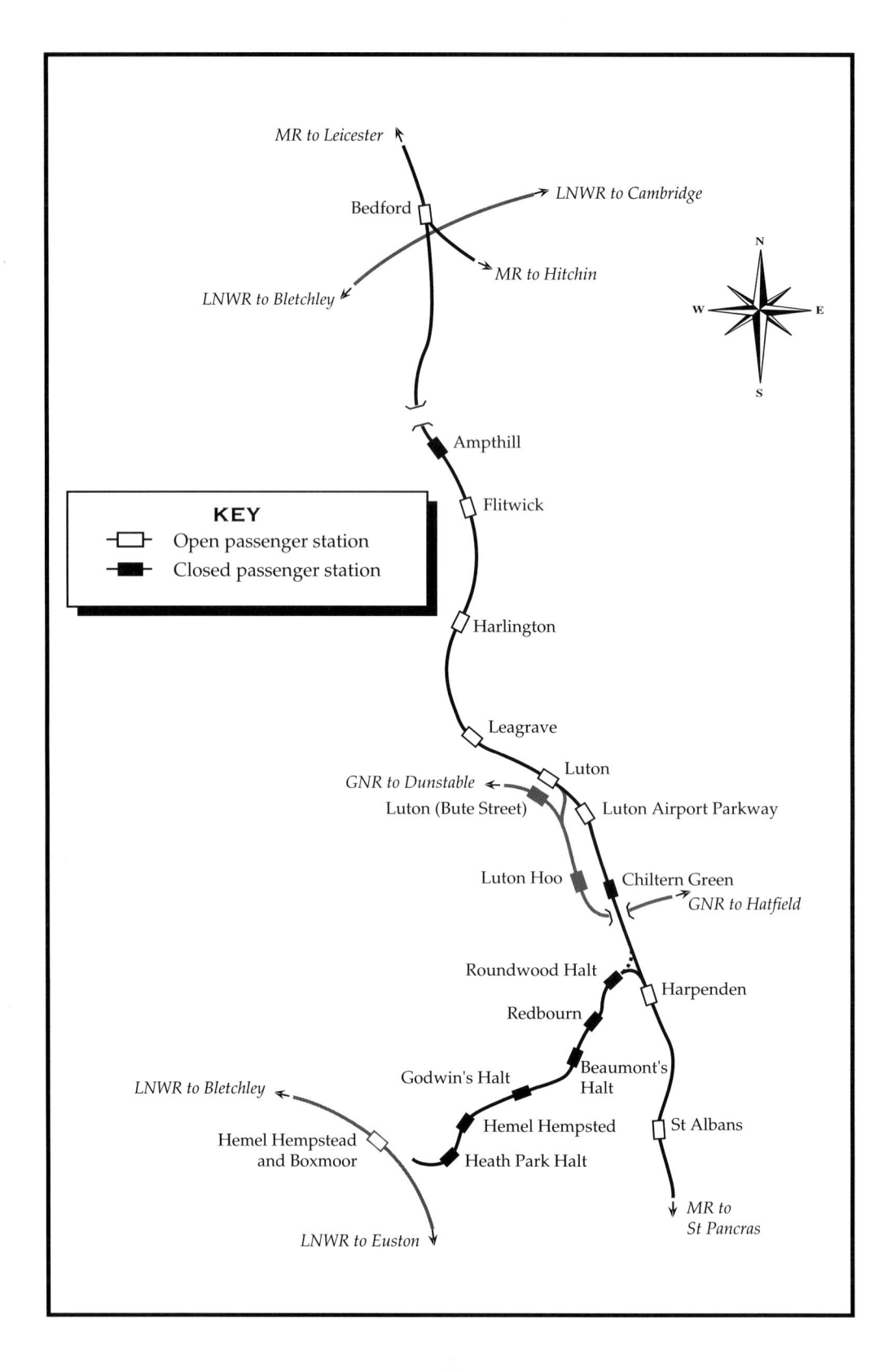

HISTORICAL BACKGROUND

THE MAIN LINE

Midland Railway trains had reached London in 1858 by means of running powers over the Great Northern Railway from Hitchin. The traffic, however, suffered from delays due to congestion on the GNR. There was also a loss of possible revenue from London coal traffic handed over to the London & North Western Railway at Rugby. With its own line to London, the MR would benefit from some 75 miles of its own haulage of this traffic. The two factors combined to make an independent Midland route to London a favourable economic proposition. On 14th October 1862, the directors of the Midland Railway resolved that *"The necessary surveys be made and plans prepared for a Line of Railway from some point on the Leicester to Hitchin Railway at or south of Bedford to London...."*. The Midland Railway (Extension to London) Act duly received Royal assent on 22nd June 1863. It was proposed originally that the Extension would diverge from the Hitchin line south of the Elstow Road overbridge at Bedford. In this event it would have been most difficult to eliminate the existing crossing on the level of the Hitchin line with the London & North Western's Bletchley line and it was decided eventually to make the junction immediately south of Bedford station even though this involved a separate crossing of the Ouse and an increase in length of the new undertaking.

With the operation of heavy coal trains in mind, the line was built with a ruling gradient in the up direction of 1 in 200 although there is about a mile of 1 in 184 just south of Bedford. From 90 ft above sea level at Bedford the line rises in 16 miles to a summit 403 ft above sea level at MP $33^{3/4}$, much of the climb being at 1 in 202. Undulations for the next 11 miles lead to a descent largely at 1 in 176 which continues through St Albans. Although built as a double track line, quadrupling was provided for from the start. Sufficient land was purchased and some work on underbridges for the goods lines was undertaken initially. The main passenger buildings at the intermediate stations were all on the down side with the goods yards on the up side, each set back to allow room for a pair of goods lines to be laid down between the platforms and the yard. Flitwick, added later, with a yard on the down side, was an excepton to this rule. On 2nd July 1867, the Board had resolved that *"The General Manager be authorised to have the Telegraph Apparatus necessary to carry out the block system of Signalling Trains constructed on the Extension.....".* Absolute block working was therefore in use from the first, although a much modified system was introduced later for the goods lines.

Through goods trains to London commenced using the line south of Bedford on 9th September 1867. Initially, they ran at night with the contractors still having possession during the day. At that stage work on the intermediate stations was still incomplete and local goods services did not commence until December of that year. The first local passenger trains from Bedford ran on the Extension on 13th July 1868. The City branch was used with Moorgate Street serving as the London terminus. Succesive Board of Trade inspections postponed the opening of St Pancras until 1st October 1868. On that date the longer distance passenger trains were diverted at Bedford from the Hitchin line and the new Extension was then fully in use.

While the line was still under construction there were a request for an additional station to be provided at Flitwick, which eventually opened on 2nd May 1870.

Widening commenced with the opening of an up goods line from Leagrave to Luton on 13th October 1875. From then piecemeal provision of the additional lines continued with the up goods always being given priority. Major engineering works were required for the crossing of the river Lea at Hyde Mill near Chiltern Green and the boring of the second Ampthill tunnel. The widening in general was on the east side of the formation but the new tunnel was sited on the west side and the original pair of lines were diverted through it to become the fast lines with the new goods lines contained in the old tunnel. Quadrupling was completed on 28th July 1895 with the opening of the down goods line throughout from Harlington to Elstow, about three miles south of Bedford. The quadrupling enabled an enormous coal traffic to be carried on the goods lines which for many years were worked by the Midland's "Telegraph Bell System". This system enabled a signalman to warn and then admit trains to an already occupied section. It allowed trains to queue one behind another at locations where the working reverted to absolute block such as the slow lines through Bedford station. The new lines were worked as goods lines throughout until 1906 when absolute block working was introduced between St Albans and Harpenden Junction and up slow platforms were provided at Harpenden and St Albans. This allowed stopping passenger trains to use the slow lines as far north as Harpenden Junction.

There were few running connectons between the passsenger and goods lines initially. Additional junctions were, however, installed at Leagrave, Harlington and Millbrook in 1913.

In the grouping of 1923, the line was absorbed by the London Midland & Scottish Railway and remained as such until nationalisation in 1948, when it became part of the London Midland Region of British Railways.

Apart from the connections referred to above, the signalling and track layouts saw no major changes for 65 years from the completion of the widening until the introduction of the DMU service in January 1960. A major munitions factory was built for WW2 at Wilshampstead between Elstow and Houghton Conquest boxes. Extensive sidings and a passenger terminus which could be accessed directly in the up direction formed part of the works. Special trains for munition workers ran to Wilshampstead from Bedford. For the DMU interval service the goods lines were converted to slow lines with absolute block working. New up slow platforms with extended footbridges were provided at Luton, Leagrave, Harlington and Flitwick. The previous back platform or bay road at Luton was extended at the north end to become the down slow platform line. A facing crossover at Bedford Junction enabled terminating DMUs to run into the up platform line from the down direction. At Luton South box, a connection to the former Great Northern line was opened in 1966. This provided access to the Luton-Dunstable section after the closure of the route from Hatfield. Such a connection had been authorised by the original Act for the Extension but it was never provided. It was removed in 1989 after traffic to Dunstable had ceased. The 1970s saw traffic on the route at a low ebb. Gradually the intermediate signal boxes were closed with consequent longer block sections. For instance, from 1973 only Millbrook box remained to break the nine miles between Flitwick and Kempston Road Junction, a situation unthinkable today when the route is operating at near capacity at peak times.

Much larger changes took place when the route was electrified in the early 1980s. The layout at Luton was again modified. The up slow platform was rebuilt as an island with the inner face mostly used by terminating trains. Manual block signalling was replaced throughout by track circuit block with colour light signals under the control of West Hampstead Power Signal Box. A reversing siding was provided at St. Albans for terminating trains. The previous junctions between fast and slow lines were replaced by double ladder connections with 40 mph limits. These were located on lengths of straight track south of Harpenden and north of Leagrave and Flitwick. An up slow to up fast connection was provided at Luton. At what was now termed Bedford South Junction, but actually located south of the previous Kempston Road Junction, the connections were arranged to permit parallel down fast to down slow and up slow to up fast movements with 50 mph limits. Bi-directional working on the slow lines was provided for between Bedford South Junction and Bedford station and it is not unusual for trains to pass on this section while running on the right hand tracks. The changeover of the area to control from West Hampstead took place between October 1979 and November 1980, the final manual boxes to remain open being Kempston Road Junction, Bedford Junction and Bedford North, all of which were closed on 2nd November 1980.

Under the privatisation scheme introduced by the Conservative government of the day, the franchise for operating the Midland main line was awarded to the National Express Group plc, which began operating under a ten year contract on 28th April 1996.

The following year, GOVIA plc acquired a seven year, one month franchise for working the Thameslink services linking Bedford with London and Brighton and commenced operation on 2nd March 1997.

THE HEMEL HEMPSTED BRANCH

This was built by the Hemel Hempsted & London & North Western Railway Co. **The spelling *Hempsted* was subsequently perpetuated by the MR and is used herein.** An Act of 14th July 1863 authorised a line from Hemel to a connection with the LNWR at Boxmoor "*....by means of a siding at such place as the LNWR agree and not otherwise*". Agreement was not achieved and although the formation was levelled into the LNWR yard, rails reached only to Boxmoor gas works. An Act of 16th July 1866 extended the authorised line in a north easterly direction through Redbourn to join the Great Northern Railway at Harpenden. Limited financial resources resulted in a long struggle to complete the construction. This culminated in an agreement to hand over the line to the MR at a fixed rental of £ 3,750 per annum. The line was completed not to the GNR but to a junction with the MR north of Harpenden facing towards Luton. The MR obtained Parliamentary authority to work the line which was opened on 16th July 1877 with an intermediate station at Redbourn. The HH&LNWR Co. was dissolved and vested in the MR in 1886 and the junction at Harpenden was altered to face south from 2nd July 1888. New halts at Beaumont's, Godwin's and Heath Park were opened on 9th August 1905 when a railmotor service was instituted. Beaumont's and Godwin's were between Redbourn and Hemel Hempsted, Heath Park was reached by a portion of line beyond Hemel

VII

Hempsted previously only used for goods traffic. Roundwood Halt, between Harpenden and Redbourn was opened by the LMS on 8th August 1927. The line was worked by a train staff without fixed signals. All points were controlled by Annett's key. It was unusual in that a passenger service terminated at a halt.

Passenger services on the branch were *"temporarily suspended"* on 16th June 1947 but were never reinstated. Goods traffic, which had ceased beyond Godwin's Depot on 1st July 1963, was, from 2nd March 1964, confined to the traffic of the Hemel Hempstead Lightweight Concrete Co. at Claydale sidings west of Beaumont's Halt. The company, producers of "Hemelite" building blocks using fly ash from power stations, took over from BR the portion of the branch from Claydale sidings to a point near Harpenden Junction 30 yards west of MP 25½ on 29th April 1968, exchanging traffic there with BR. The last delivery of ash was made on 27th June 1979 and the junction at Harpenden was severed as part of the electrification process. Ironically, a connection at the western extremity of the line, from Boxmoor goods yard to Boxmoor gas works was in use from 31st August 1959 to 1st April 1960 to enable the latter to be supplied with coal.

Hemel Hempsted branch service 7th October 1946 - 4th May 1947.

PASSENGER SERVICES

The first passenger service commenced between Bedford and Moorgate Street on 13th July 1868, St Pancras being incomplete. The initial timetable shows that the trains started and finished their day's duties at Luton. "Engine Houses" at Bedford and St Albans to hold four engines each were not authorised until 31st March 1868 and were unlikely to have been ready for the opening. St Pancras was opened on 1st October 1868 and main line trains which previously had run to King's Cross via Hitchin were diverted at Bedford to the new terminus.

The growth of passenger traffic in Midland Railway in days is best illustrated by the records of the numbers of passengers booked at each station shown on the table opposite.

By 1883 Luton had a morning train at 7.17a.m. to St Pancras calling at all stations to Hendon except Chiltern

STATION	No. of Passengers Booked					
	1873	1883	1893	1903	1913	1922
Bedford	116,613	143,696	180,929	226,652	229,023	230,808
Ampthill	14,279	20,472	24,900	22,356	24,220	20,825
Flitwick	11,234	14,275	17,999	22,500	31,212	28,298
Harlington	10,794	14,764	15,729	18,813	22,297	20,012
Leagrave	6,856	20,648	19,843	31,006	24,948	22,533
Luton	86,965	136,857	147,482	200,063	263,385	259,871
Chiltern Green	4,295	7,908	7,379	7,368	4,189	3,728
Hemel Hempsted	-	7,339	11,110	16,546	16,409	13,350
Redbourn	-	7,375	12,291	14,517	11,936	11,532
Harpenden	29,678	41,522	63,684	97,661	136,638	104,771
St Albans	55,468	77,530	108,239	171,034	208,444	197,498

Green. This was followed by the 7.0 a.m from Bedford, all stations to Mill Hill. Bedford also had the benefit of calls by overnight trains from Scotland at 6.41 a.m and 7.25 a.m (Mondays excepted) which provided non-stop services to St Pancras although regular business travel over such a distance would then have been rare. The records show that in general traffic at the towns grew at a faster rate than that at the smaller stations. The latter, however, were well served. In 1913, before the disruption of World War I, nine up trains called daily at Harlington and Leagrave with one more at Ampthill and two more at Flitwick. Even Chiltern Green, where only 13 passengers were booked on an average day, had seven up stopping trains. Non-stop times to St Pancras were 35 to 40 minutes from Luton and 55 to 62 minutes from Bedford. Luton was served daily by slip carriages off three up expresses from Manchester.

Recovery from the effects of World War I was slow and it was not until 1937 that the introduction of "XL Limit" timings brought about 30 minute bookings to St Pancras from Luton and a 52 minute run from Bedford. In practice, 30 minutes from Luton left little or no margin for checks. Cut short by WWII, the timings of 1937 were never repeated with steam traction. Heavier loads and coal of variable quality meant that post-war accelerations demanded large scale piloting of expresses. Local workings stagnated until a DMU interval service was instituted in January 1960. This had hourly off peak workings from Bedford, calling at all stations to Elstree, and from Luton, calling at all stations. Timings from St Pancras were 70 minutes to Bedford and 54½ minutes to Luton. Comparable 1958 steam timings were 95 and 71 minutes respectively.

The interval service was a great improvement but the units (Class 127) did not age well and the announcement, in November 1976, that the line from Moorgate and St Pancras to Bedford was to be electrified was welcomed. The full service was intended to be introduced in May 1982. A dispute over single manning and teething troubles with the new Class 317 units delayed the commencement of the full service for seventeen months until October 1983, during which time the ailing 127s had to carry on, supplemented at peak times by tired Class 45s hauling Mk1 coaches. The first basic timetable of the full electric service was two Bedford/St Pancras and two Luton/Moorgate trains per hour.

A further revolution in the service occurred on 16th May 1988 with the commencement of through running to stations south of the Thames via the reopened Snow Hill link. The Class 317 units were replaced by Class 319s which are able to operate on either 25kV AC or 750V DC. Orpington, Sevenoaks and Guildford have all been served from Luton at times but the timetable has now settled down to Bedford/Brighton and Luton/Sutton, both at fifteen minute intervals off peak. The Sutton trains run to Streatham via Herne Hill and Tulse Hill and then alternately clockwise and anti-clockwise round the Sutton and Wimbledon loop. The frequency of the present service, with four off-peak trains per hour from Bedford, doubling to eight per hour south of Luton, is unrivalled.

BEDFORD MIDLAND ROAD
SUNDAYS

Sunday departures from Bedford Midland Road : 9th June - 14th September 1958.

THE NUMBER OF TRAINS CALLING AT BOTH ST. ALBANS AND BEDFORD, ON AT LEAST FIVE DAYS A WEEK

	Weekdays	Sundays		Weekdays	Sundays
1869	8	4	1949	23	8
1889	12	6	1969	36	17
1909	25	6	1989	52	39
1929	17	6	1999	71	56

ST. ALBANS

1. We start our journey at St. Albans, with this evocative view, looking north in 1928. Passengers stand on the island platform as 0-4-4T No 1377 prepares to depart with an up stopping train. (Stations U.K.)

2. Here we see No 1377 again, but this time the date is 9th May 1931. She has just brought in a terminating train and is being released to go to the shed. (H. C. Casserley)

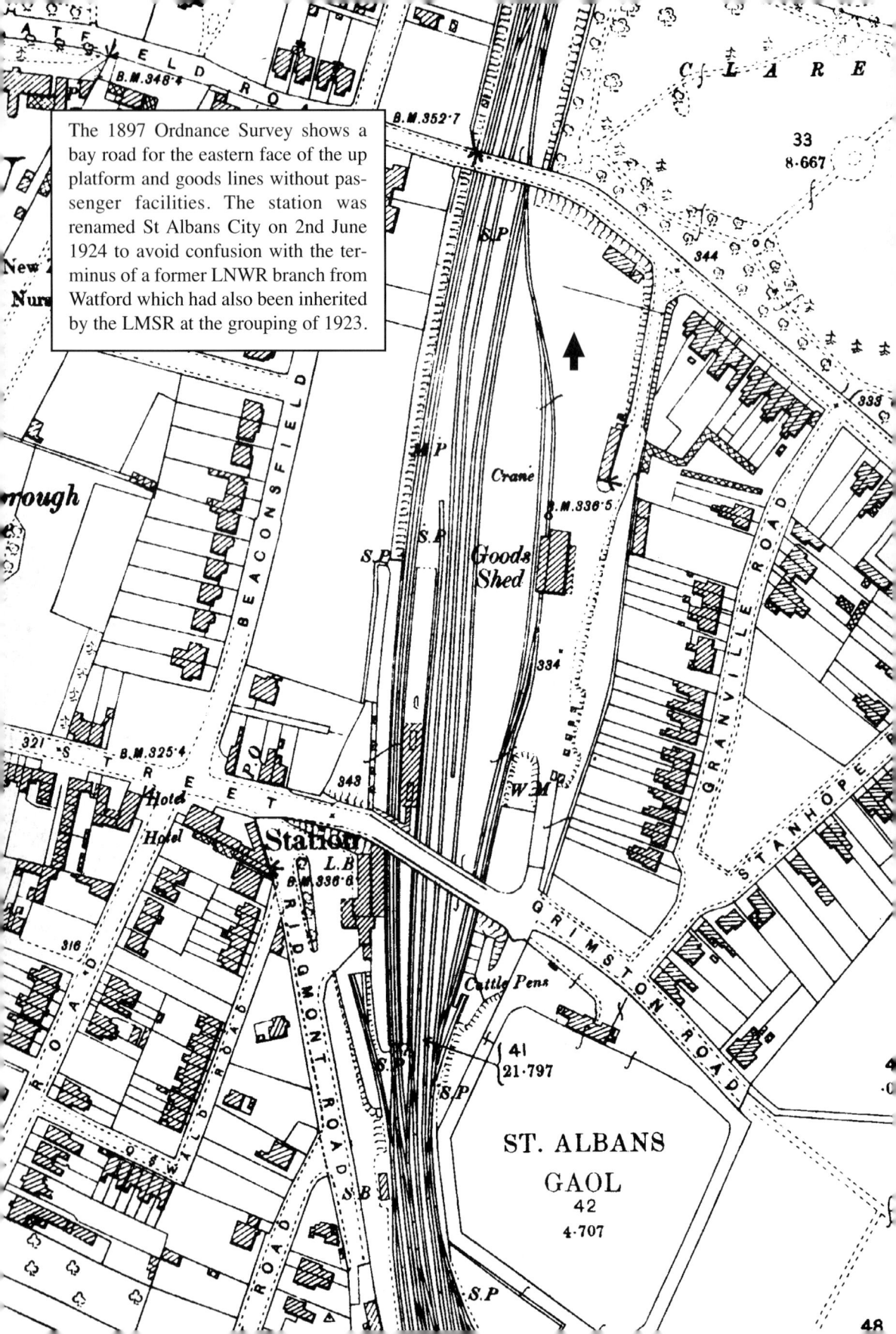

The 1897 Ordnance Survey shows a bay road for the eastern face of the up platform and goods lines without passenger facilities. The station was renamed St Albans City on 2nd June 1924 to avoid confusion with the terminus of a former LNWR branch from Watford which had also been inherited by the LMSR at the grouping of 1923.

3. Passenger activity is brisk as a St Pancras to Bedford train calls at the down fast platform on 24th May 1947. The later addition of an art deco style clock contrasts with the original ridge and furrow glazed canopy. (E. D. Bruton)

4. Standing on the island platform we look north in 1971 and see the main building on the left. The station was beginning to look a little run-down by this time, but complete reconstruction was only two years away. (Stations U.K.)

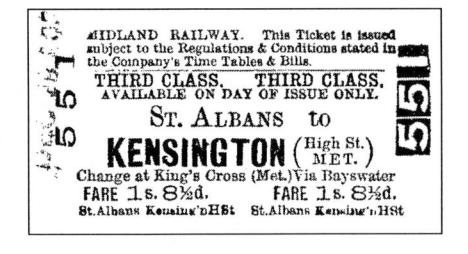

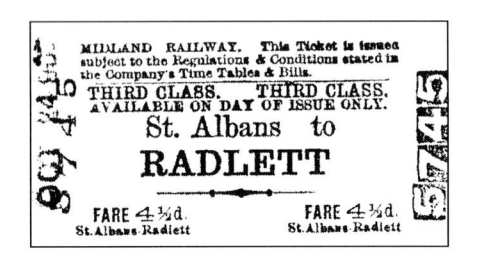

MIDLAND RAILWAY. This Ticket is issued subject to the Regulations & Conditions stated in the Company's Time Tables & Bills.
THIRD CLASS.   THIRD CLASS.
AVAILABLE ON DAY OF ISSUE ONLY.
St. Albans to
KENSINGTON (High St.) (MET.)
Change at King's Cross (Met.) Via Bayswater
FARE 1s. 8½d.   FARE 1s. 8½d.
St.Albans Kensing'nHSt   St.Albans Kensing'nHSt

MIDLAND RAILWAY. This Ticket is issued subject to the Regulations & Conditions stated in the Company's Time Tables & Bills.
THIRD CLASS.   THIRD CLASS.
AVAILABLE ON DAY OF ISSUE ONLY.
St. Albans to
RADLETT
FARE 4½d.   FARE 4½d.
St.Albans-Radlett   St.Albans-Radlett

MIDLAND RAILWAY.
This Ticket is issued subject to the Regulations & Conditions stated in the Co.'s Time Tables & Bills.
THIRD CLASS.   THIRD CLASS.
AVAILABLE ON DAY OF ISSUE ONLY.
HARPENDEN to
ST. ALBANS
FARE 5d.   FARE 5d.
Harpenden St.Albans   Harpenden St.Albans

5. The station was rebuilt in 1973, having lost its 'City' suffix on 5th May 1968. Here we stand on the up platform used by Thameslink services and look northwards in the 1980s. (D. Thompson)

6. As part of the rebuilding, a new main entrance, erected on the up side, provided direct access to the platform seen above, whilst the former goods yard was adapted to provide a car park. In this view, we look down from the road bridge towards the building which incorporates the ticket office and refreshment facilities. (D. Thompson)

7. Here we see a Midland MainLine High Speed Train, heading northwards through St. Albans on 30th April 1998. (M. Turvey)

8. The *Midland Pullman*, a forerunner of the HSTs, approaches St Albans on its inaugural up run from Manchester on 4th July 1960. (M. Joyce)

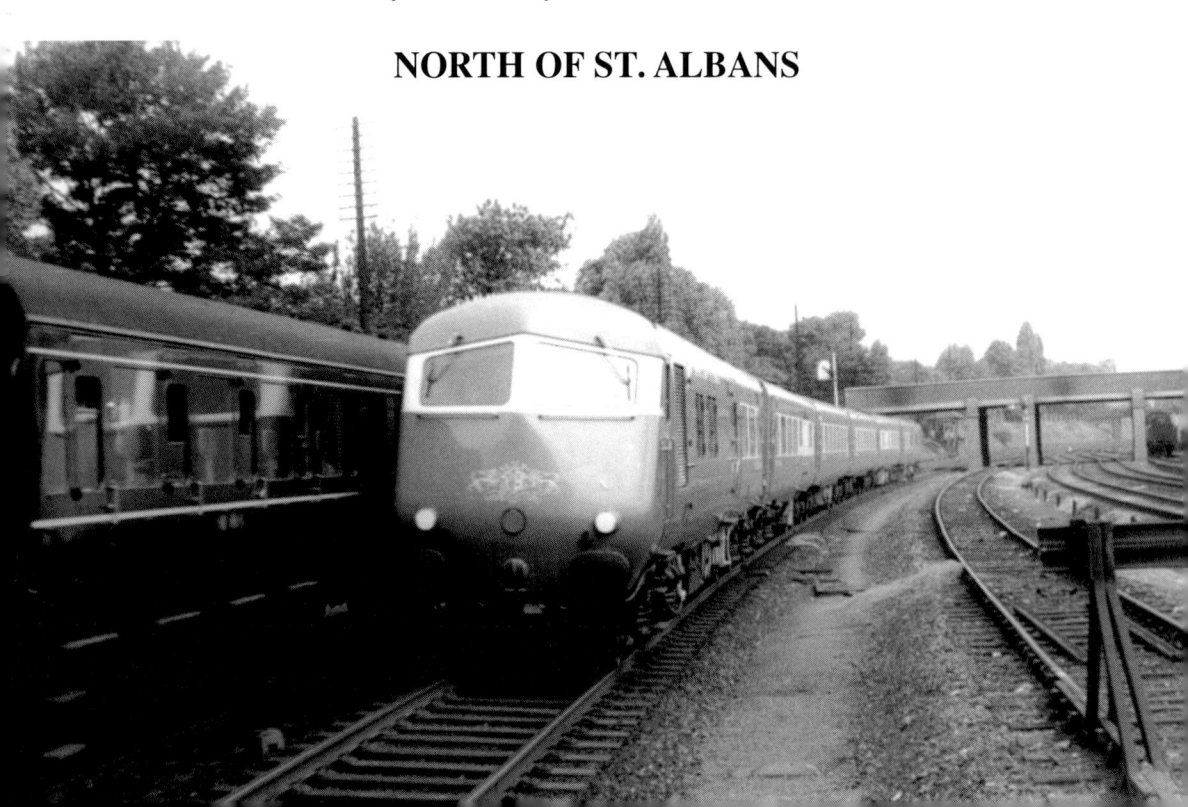

NORTH OF ST. ALBANS

SOUTH OF HARPENDEN

9. Standard Class 5MTs Nos.73001 and 73000 try their strength south of Harpenden on a test run with a vacuum fitted coal train on 26th October 1952. (E. D. Bruton)

Pages 81-83.—
   The station references to "Bedford" should read "Bedford (Mid. Road)".

Page 82—*Amend distance.*—
   Bromham—1,523 yards.
Add speed restriction.—
   Between Bedford South and Harpenden Junction except where otherwise shown—up and down goods lines—50 miles per hour.

Page 83—*Add speed restrictions.*—
   Over goods lines at North end of Harlington Station—up and down—40 miles per hour.
   Over goods lines at south end of Leagrave Station—up and down—30 miles per hour.
   Over goods lines through Luton Station—up and down—30 miles per hour.
   Over goods lines at south end of Chiltern Green Station—up and down—35 miles per hour.
   Between Luton and Chiltern Green, 30¼ and 28 mile posts—up and down main—75 miles per hour.
   Between St. Albans and Napsbury—over curves between 20 and 18½ mile posts—up and down main—75 miles per hour.
Sandridge:—
   Amend down fast and down slow line engine whistle:—
      p 4 Stopping at Luton for water or traffic (not passenger trains).

Supplement No 1 to the Working Timetable Sectional Appendix, LMSR Midland Division, March 1937.

HARPENDEN

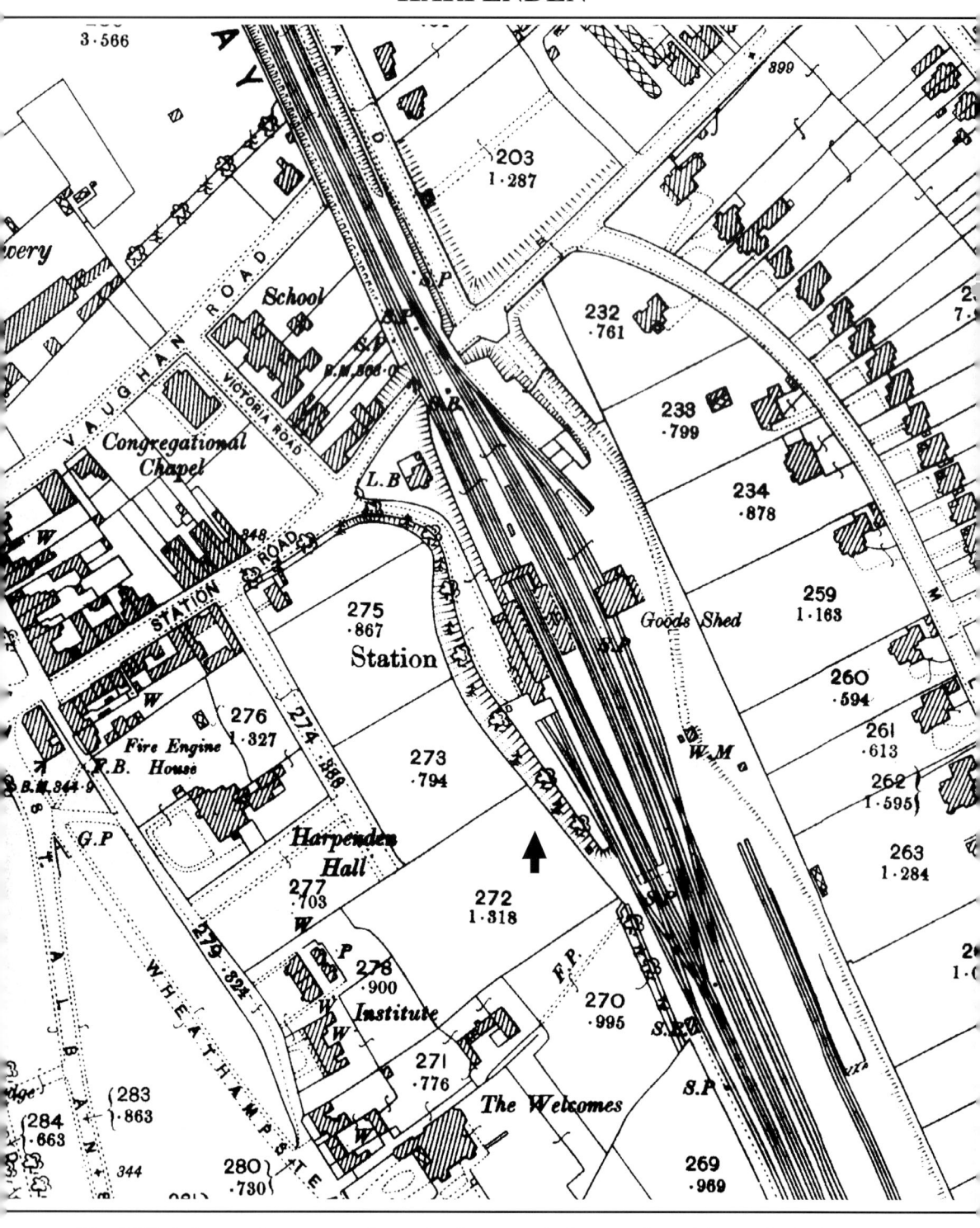

The 1897 Ordnance Survey map shows the then two-platform station with a back-platform road. Development in nearby Milton Road comprises detached houses in large plots.

10. A double headed up express passes the station in 1902. An up slow platform was not added until 1906. (G. W. Goslin collection)

11. The station exterior in the 1930s. The stationmaster's house faces the approach road. (The Lens of Sutton Collection)

12. An up express headed by Class 5 No. 44839 approaches the station in about 1950. The site of the Hemel Hempsted bay can be seen on the left. (E. D. Bruton)

13. A 1953 view looking north from the island platform between the up fast and down slow lines. The only structure of those seen which now survives is the original booking hall on the extreme left. (Locomotive & General Railway Photographs)

14. We look south from the down fast platform in about 1960. The difference between the two spans of the footbridge is due to the 1906 extension on the left to serve the up slow platform. The premises had been renamed Harpenden Central on 25th September 1950 to avoid confusion with a former GNR station which also served the town. This closed on 26th April 1965 however, so the 'Central' suffix became surplus and was dropped from 18th April 1966. (The Lens of Sutton Collection)

15. Looking from the up slow platform we see the uncomfortable juxtaposition on the down fast platform of the original station building and the new footbridge in September 2001. (G. W. Goslin)

HEMEL HEMPSTED BRANCH

16. We look north to see the MR Harpenden Junction box with its southwards view limited by the bridge pier. The Hemel Hempsted branch, which opened to passenger traffic on 16th July 1877, diverges to the left. The site is on the summit of a well defined hump in the undulations between St Albans and Leagrave. The junction marked the change from passenger and goods lines northwards to fast and slow lines southwards. A common sight was a queue of coal trains awaiting their turn to enter the absolute block territory to the south. (F. W. Shuttleworth)

17. The MR box at Harpenden Junction was replaced in 1957 by a structure with a flat roof and a brick base, seen on 10th May 1978. (P. E. B. Butler)

18. The Hemel Hempsted train stands in the newly provided bay platform at Harpenden in 1906. A 4-4-0T on exchange from the Midland & Great Northern Joint Railway heads a converted Pullman car. (G. W. Goslin collection)

ROUNDWOOD HALT

19. Roundwood Halt was a late addition, not being opened until 8th August 1927 when traffic was already in decline. This view, taken after closure, is looking towards Harpenden. (G. Woodward collection)

REDBOURN

20. Redbourn was the only intermediate station on the Hemel Hempsted branch and opened with the line in 1877. There were fearsome gradients between the station and Harpenden junction including a quarter mile stretch of 1 in 37 against down trains. Up trains had to tackle over half a mile of 1 in 39 soon after leaving Redbourn. (The Lens of Sutton Collection)

The Ordnance Survey map of 1898.

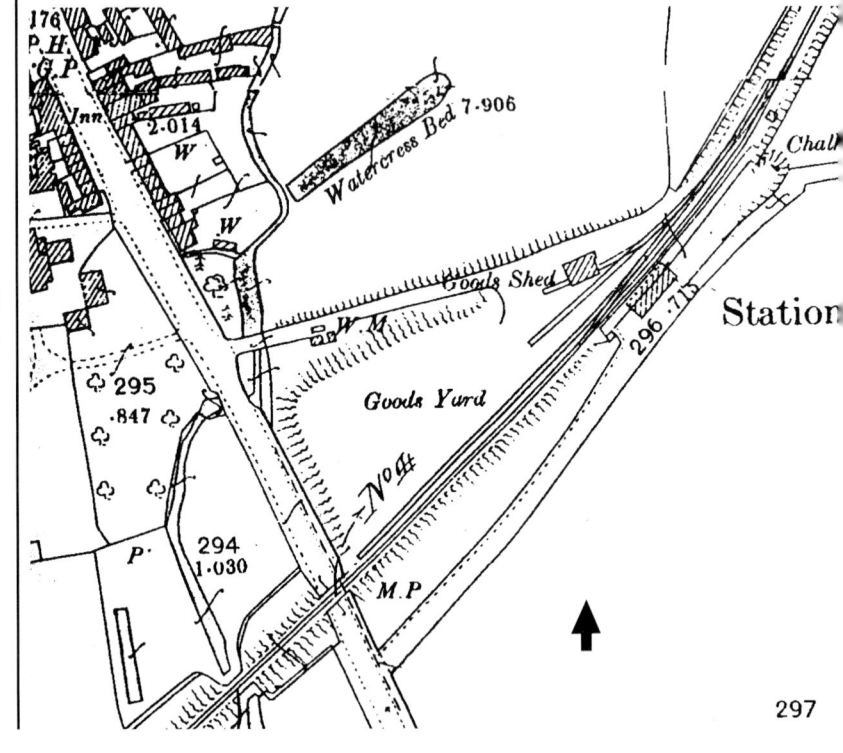

BEAUMONT'S HALT

21. The LMS 'hawkseye' nameboard still stands at Beaumont's Halt in May 1957, ten years after the last passenger train called, although a daily goods train still ran on the branch in each direction, usually worked by an Ivatt Class 4MT 2-6-0 from St Albans. The halt had opened on 9th August 1905. (R. A. S. Marketing)

Miles				771 Stopping Freight to Harpenden	772 E. & R.	773 Stopping Freight to Harpenden	774 Stopping Freight to Harpenden	775
				S		SO Stops at Chaydale Brick and Tile Co.'s Sid. when required	S	
				a.m.	p.m.	p.m.	p.m.	
0		GAS WORKS SIDS. ....dep.		9 45	..	..	..	..
¼		Heath Park		10 30	4 40	5 15	7 30	..
1½		Hemel Hempsted ....?	arr.	10 35	4 45	5 20	7 35	..
			dep.	10 45	..	5 30	7 45	..
5¼		Redbourn	arr.	11 5	..	5 55	8 10	..
			dep.	11 35	..	6 5	8 20	..
8¼	832	HARPENDEN JUNCTION?		11*47	..	6*18	8*27	..

Miles				781 6.35 a.m. Stop's Freight from Harpenden	782 Mineral	784 Stops at Chaydale Brick and Tile Co.'s Sid. and Godwin's Siding when required.	785 1.10 p.m. Stop's Freight from Harpenden	786 2.40 a.m. Stop's Freight from Harpenden
						S	SO	
				a.m.	a.m.	p.m.	p.m.	
0	840	HARPENDEN JUNCTION?		6*35	..	3*13	3*48	..
3		Redbourn	arr.	..	..	3 22	3 52	..
			dep.	..	..	3 32	4 2	..
7¼		Hemel Hempsted ....?	arr.	7 0	..	4 7	4 37	..
			dep.	..	9 25	4 17	4 47	..
8		Heath Park		..	..	4 22	4 52	..
8¼		GAS WORKS SIDS. ....arr.		..	9 35	..	..	..

LMSR Freight Service Working Timetable 1934.

GODWIN'S HALT

22. Situated at the summit of the branch, Godwin's Halt was 469 ft above sea level, the highest point reached by the Midland Railway south of Nottingham and Derby. It opened on 9th August 1905 and was approached on gradients of 1 in 39 in either direction. (G. Woodward collection)

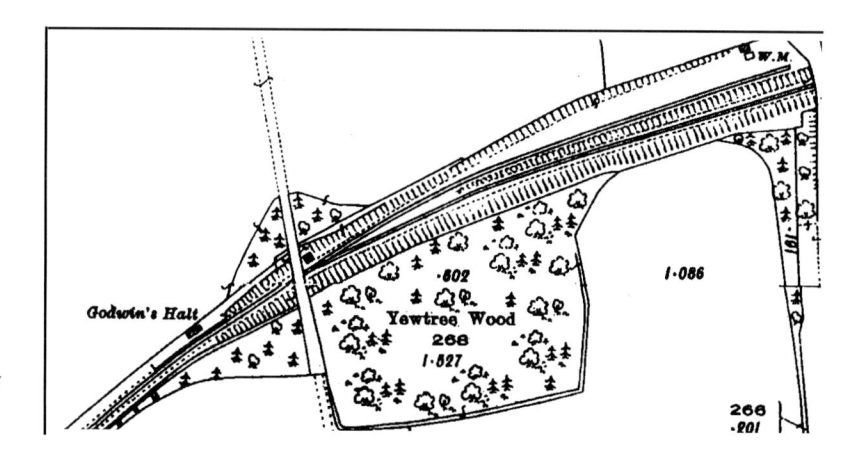

Ordnance Survey Map of 1925.

HEMEL HEMPSTED

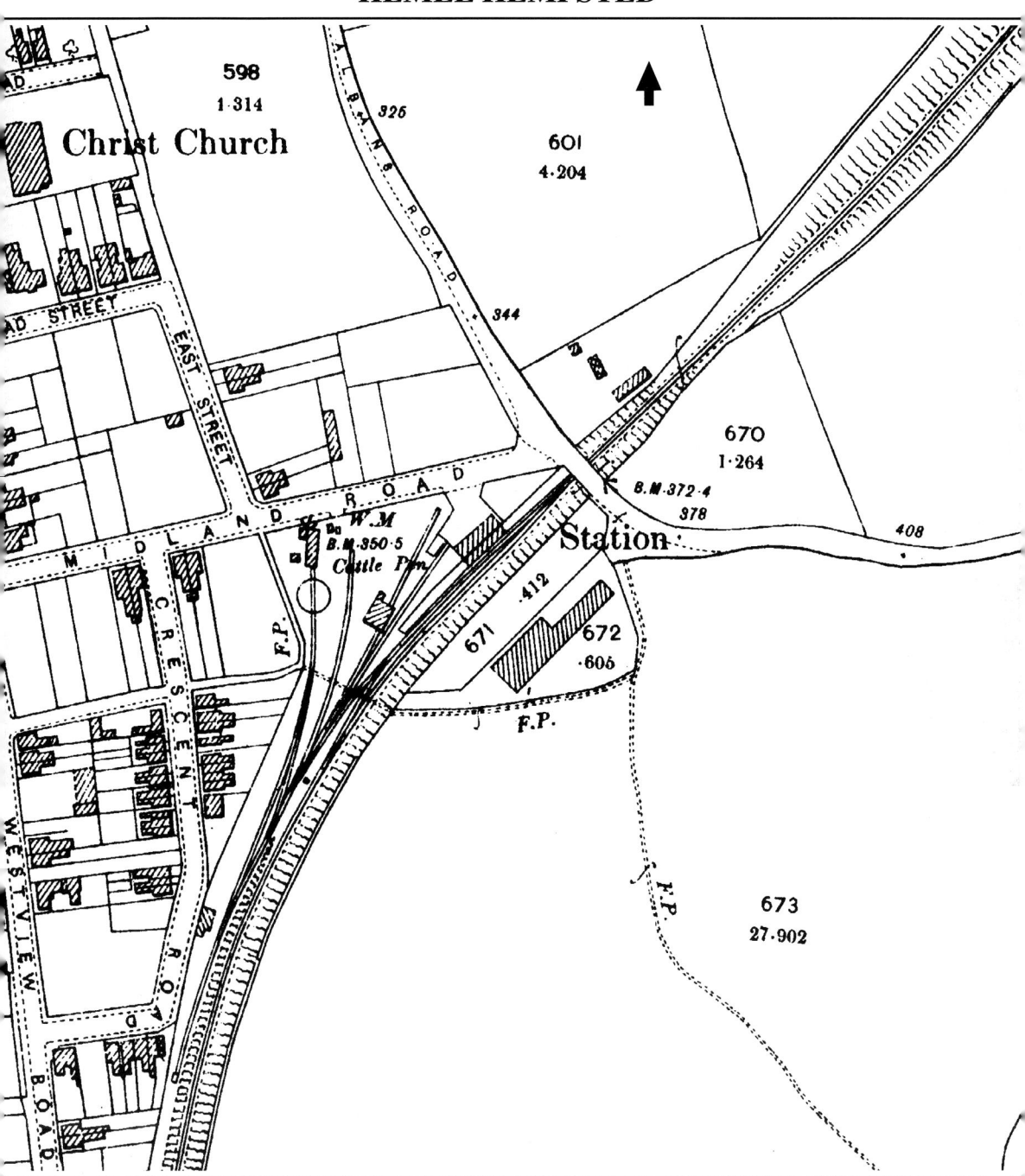

The station opened as Hemel Hempstead, but the spelling was changed to *'Hempsted'* on 1st June 1880. This 1897 Ordnance Survey shows the facilities provided at Hemel Hempsted, which although limited, included a turntable and a loop opposite the single platform. To the south of the station, the branch continued towards Heath Park Halt and the intended junction with the LNWR main line.

23. The station is seen about 1910 with stock including a converted Pullman car stabled in the cattle pen road. The station building and canopy is similar to that at Redbourn. Immediately after leaving for Harpenden, trains faced about three quarters of a mile at 1 in 39 to Godwin's Halt. (The Lens of Sutton Collection)

24. Passenger services were withdrawn from the branch on 16th June 1947, but the station remained standing for some time afterwards. In this view, dating from May 1959, the building appears to be intact despite twelve years of closure. Goods traffic was not flourishing at the time and the row of vans are probably stored. (R. A. S. Marketing)

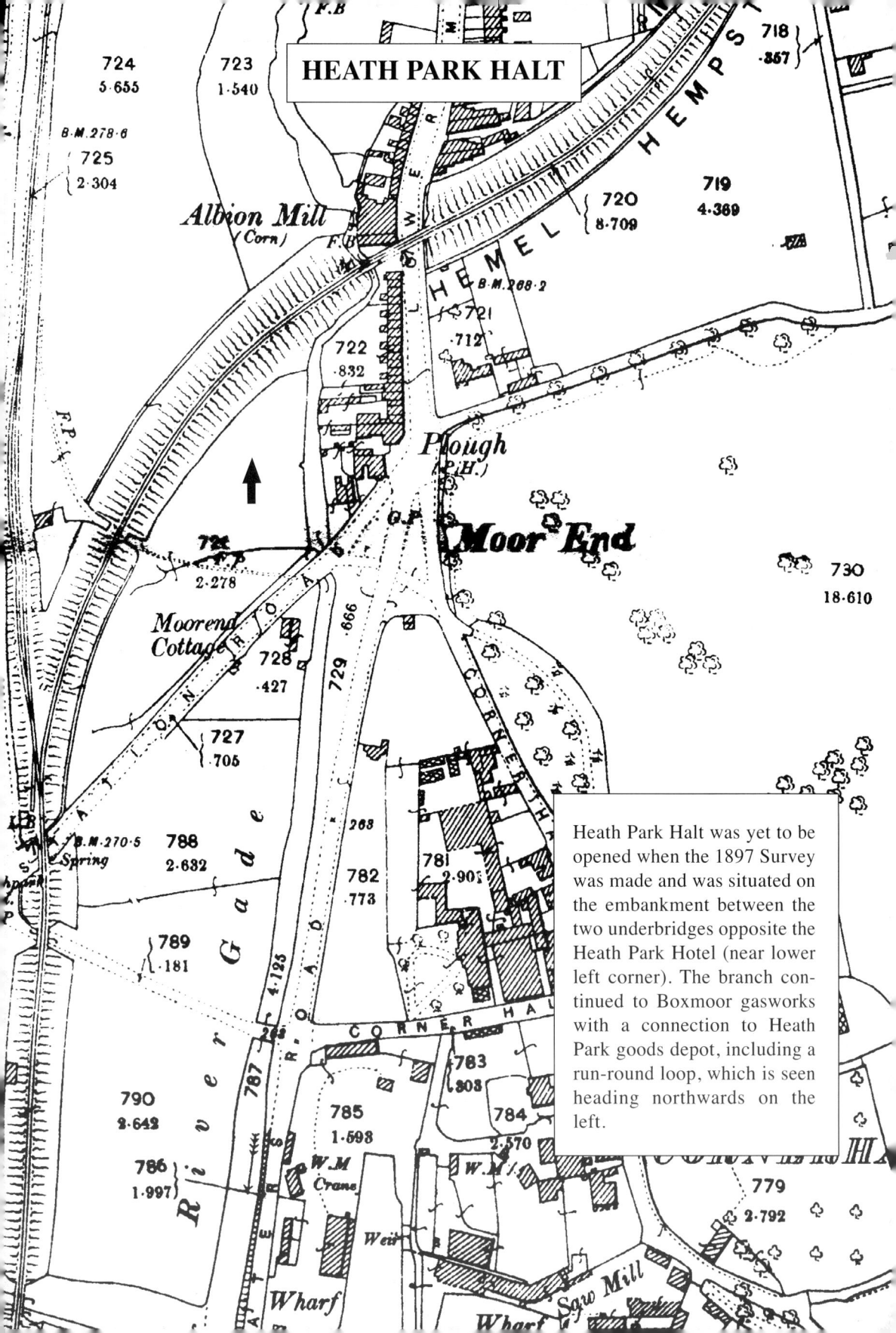

HEATH PARK HALT

Heath Park Halt was yet to be opened when the 1897 Survey was made and was situated on the embankment between the two underbridges opposite the Heath Park Hotel (near lower left corner). The branch continued to Boxmoor gasworks with a connection to Heath Park goods depot, including a run-round loop, which is seen heading northwards on the left.

25. A 4-4-0T and converted Pullman car stands at the halt, which opened on 9th August 1905 and would remain the passenger terminus. On the left is the Heath Park Hotel. (The Lens of Sutton Collection)

Hemel Hempsted Branch.

Owen's siding:—

Trains running from Redbourn to Hemel Hempsted must not attach or detach any vehicles at Owen's siding.

Claydale Brick & Tile Company's siding:—

To prevent the possibility of any vehicle running away towards Redbourn from the Claydale Brick & Tile Company's siding, no vehicle of a train going towards Hemel Hempsted must be allowed to stand upon the main line at the siding without the engine being attached. The rear portion of all trains going towards Hemel Hempsted, which have to attach or detach traffic at this siding, must be placed in the siding provided for the purpose, and the points in the main line must remain open for the siding during the time such trains are attaching or detaching traffic.

Trains running from Redbourn to Hemel Hempsted must not attach or detach any vehicle at the connection at the Redbourn end of the siding.

Godwin's siding:—

All wagons going from Hemel Hempsted to Godwin's siding must be taken in front of the engine with a Guard's brake, in which a Guard must ride, in front of them; and all wagons going from Godwin's siding to Hemel Hempsted must be taken behind the engine with a Guard's brake, in which a Guard must ride, in the rear of them.

Hemel Hempsted:—

All trains and engines approaching Hemel Hempsted from Harpenden must be brought to a stand at Hemel Hempsted Station platform.

Heath Park Depôt:—

The gates of the public road level crossing, near to Heath Park Depôt, must always be kept locked across the railway, except when required to be opened for a Midland train or engine to pass, and the key must be kept in the weighing machine house at the Depôt.

During shunting operations at Heath Park Depôt, the gates must be kept locked across the roadway, except when required to be placed across the railway to allow the road traffic to pass.

The Sidings Porter at Heath Park Depôt will be held responsible for the opening and closing of the gates.

All trains and engines running to Heath Park Depôt and from the gas works sidings must be brought to a stand before reaching the catch point to allow the Guard to unlock the point.

Instructions respecting working of Auto Car on Hemel Hempsted Branch:—

Auto cars to be dealt with as trains:—

The auto cars must, when conveying passengers, be accompanied by a Guard, and must carry the usual tail and side lamps, and one head lamp, and must be dealt with as an ordinary passenger train.

Auto cars run light:—

When the auto cars are not conveying passengers, it will not be necessary to provide a Guard, but they must be treated as light engines.

Edges of platforms at Halts to be whitewashed:—

The edges of the platforms at the Halts will be kept whitewashed to the width of one foot from the edge, and the platforms at the Halts will be kept clean by the Permanent Way staff.

Gates at Halts:—

The Permanent Way staff to examine daily the springs of the gates at the Halts, and immediately report any defect.

The Guards must take care before leaving the Halts that the gates leading to the platforms are properly secured.

MR Appendix to Working Timetable : July 1913.

SOUTH OF CHILTERN GREEN

26. Kentish Town's Compound No.41117 crosses the bridge over the ex-GNR Hatfield to Luton branch with the 2.08 p.m. Bedford to St Pancras on 28th July 1951. (E. D. Bruton)

27. Increased loads and post-war coal posed problems for the Jubilees when Midland line expresses were accelerated in the 1950s. Much piloting was resorted to, usually with Class 2P 4-4-0s. We see No.40452 assisting Jubilee No.45655 *Keith* on a down Manchester express approaching Chiltern Green on 31st August 1954. (R. Cullup collection)

28. At East Hyde, south of Chiltern Green, the original tracks, now the fast lines, cross the Luton to Wheathampstead road and the River Lea by a series of brick arches. The later goods, now slow, lines of 1894 are carried by the massive girder spans seen in this 1989 view. (G. W. Goslin)

Midland Railway Appendix to Working Timetable July 1913.

CHILTERN GREEN

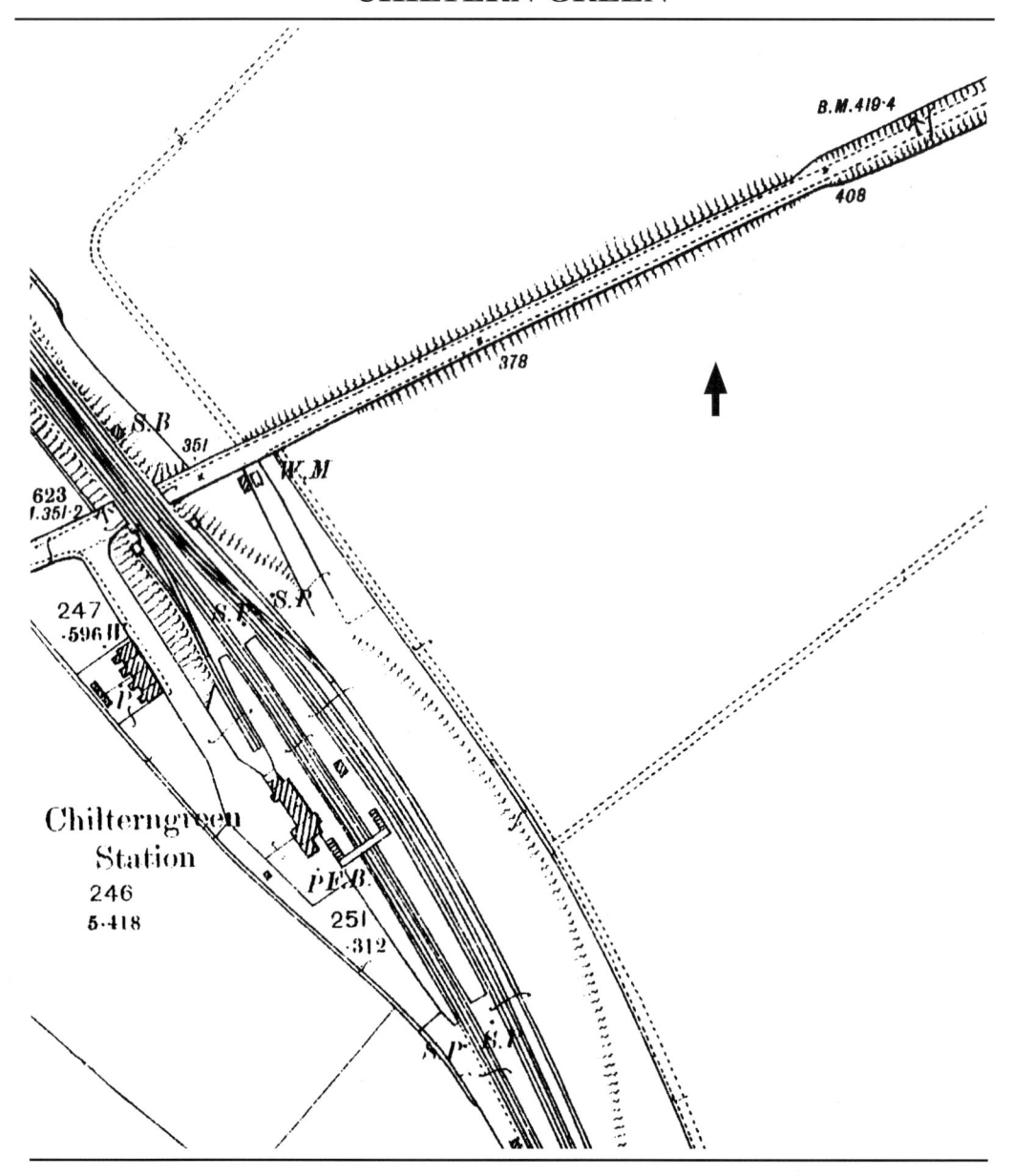

Chiltern Green opened with the line on 13th July 1868. From 1877 to 1888 the station served as a junction for London passengers using the Hemel Hempsted branch. It was, however, remote from villages and saw little patronage after the branch junction was altered to face south. On 1st December 1891, it was renamed 'Chiltern Green (For Luton Hoo)' possibly in recognition of the large country house, Luton Hoo, which was located just over a mile distant, but more likely to emphasise its close proximity to a GNR station situated to the west. This had opened as 'New Mill End' and became 'Luton Hoo' on the same date as Chiltern Green received its suffix. Traffic was never heavy and its closure to passengers on 7th April 1952 was not unexpected. The platforms, footbridge and up-side shelter were subsequently demolished, but the main building remained standing in 2003 and was used as a private residence.

29. Jubilee 4-6-0 No.5644 *Howe,* with a down fitted goods, is seen from the Chiltern Green footbridge on 12th July 1939. (H. C. Casserley)

30. Class 3F 0-6-0 No.3185 hauls a long train of empty wagons on the down goods line at Chiltern Green in 1939. The wall at the back of the up platform was a feature not found at other stations on the London Extension. (H. G. Clements / B. Cross collection)

31. A deserted Chiltern Green For Luton Hoo station is seen looking south on a wet day. (The Lens of Sutton Collection.)

LUTON AIRPORT PARKWAY

32. Growth in the number of people bound for Luton Airport resulted in the rare event of building a completely new station. This was opened on 25th November 1999 by H.M. The Queen who travelled in a reserved portion of a 319 set at 10.28 from London Bridge. Perhaps this spared Her Majesty the view of the unadorned frontage which is seen here from the top of the car park. The building of completely new stations are rare events which deserve architecture of distinction. Charles Holden designed some notable examples for the extensions of London's Underground in the 1930s. In comparison, Luton Airport Parkway seems to have relapsed into anonymity. (G. W. Goslin)

33. There is a high rise from road level to the footbridge which has to be used to reach Platforms 1 to 3. A subway would have been more convenient. (G. W. Goslin)

34. Long shelters are provided on the platforms but in this location they may prove to be rather draughty. This is the down fast platform No.4 looking north from the island. (G. W. Goslin)

35. We look south from the up slow platform No.1 on 19th June 2001. A Midland Main Line train of Class 170 units is standing in the down fast platform. (G. W. Goslin)

LUTON

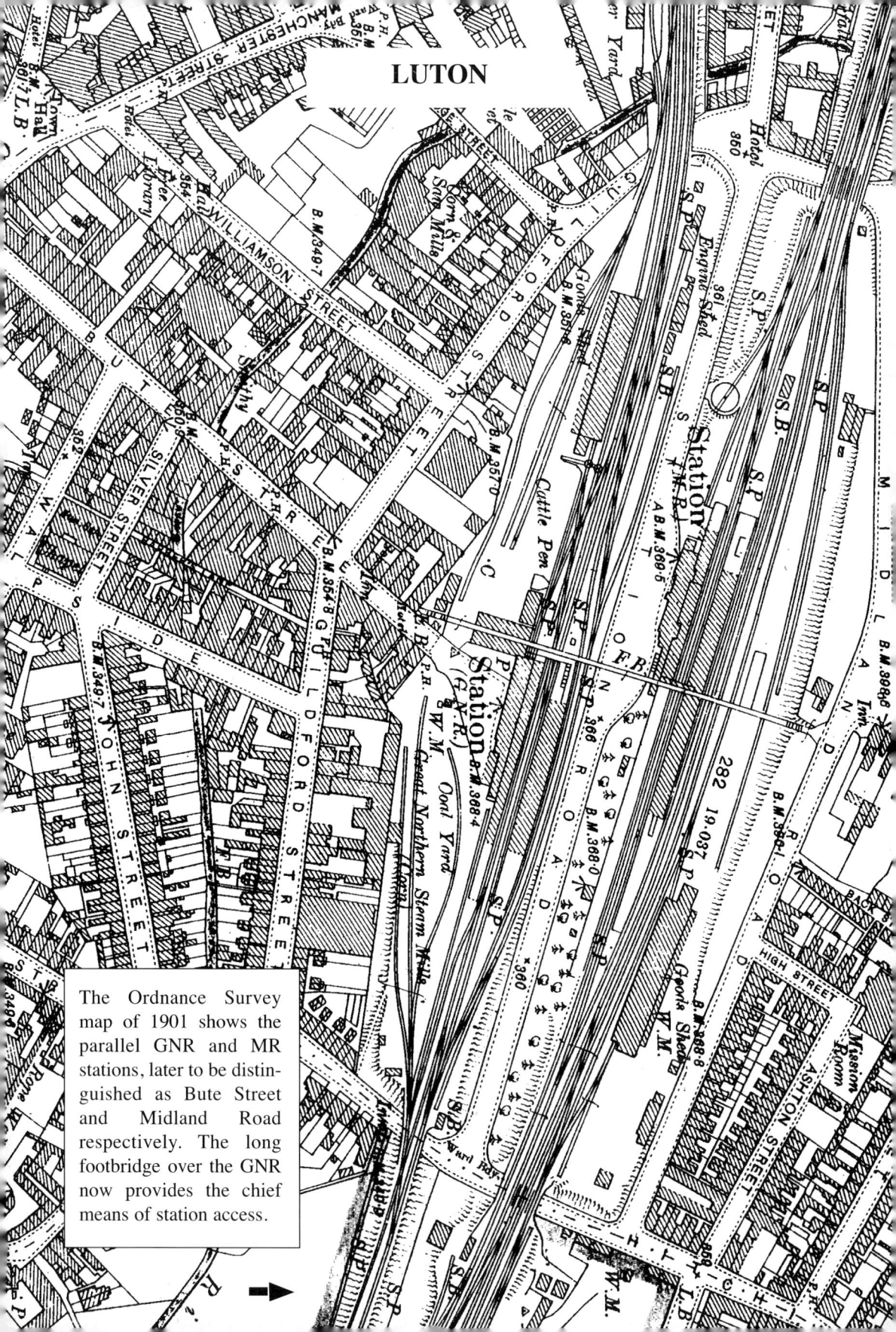

The Ordnance Survey map of 1901 shows the parallel GNR and MR stations, later to be distinguished as Bute Street and Midland Road respectively. The long footbridge over the GNR now provides the chief means of station access.

36. We look in the up direction from the down platform, probably in the 1920s, and see an ample contingent of porters awaiting the arrival of an express. (The Lens of Sutton Collection)

37. In this view, taken about 1930, we look from the railway owned Station Road towards the footbridge which crossed the LNER lines to give access to the town. The station buildings are on the left. The bus is up to date with a covered top deck and pneumatic tyres. (B. Cross collection)

38. A dramatic accident occurred to an empty wagon train in World War II. From the evidence of the photograph it appears that the train behind Garratt No.4983 had broken loose and when the locomotive came to a stand at the Luton North down goods home signal the wagons caught it up and piled up behind it. (B. Cross collection)

39. The exterior of the parcels depot was photographed in 1949. The horse drawn vehicle still retains its pre-nationalisation lettering of *Railways* in acknowledgement of the presence of both LMS and LNER in the town but the motor van has received British Railways livery. (J. Osgood)

40. 3F 0-6-0 No. 43428, a Bedford engine for at least 26 years, is seen with a down pick-up goods on 12th June 1950. (H. C. Casserley)

41. Compound 4-4-0 No.41181 calls at Luton with a Bedford to St Pancras train in about 1957. The station was renamed Luton Midland Road on 25th September 1950 to avoid confusion with the adjoining ex-GNR premises which became 'Luton Bute Street' on the same date. (J. Osgood)

42. Fowler Class 4MT 2-6-4T 2-6-4T No.42329 takes water before departing with a stopping train to St Pancras in the late 1950s. The train is standing in the up bay, now the site of the down slow platform road. The goods warehouse is seen in the background. (J. Osgood)

43. In 1937 a major rebuilding of the passenger facilities was commenced. The platform plan was unaltered but the buildings were replaced. We see the new road level entrance looking north in about 1960 from the footbridge which spanned both LMS and LNER lines. A new booking office at bridge level became the main entrance to the station. (J. Osgood)

44. A 1960s view in the same direction as picture 36 showing the late 1930s canopies and the booking hall over the lines. The up slow platform provided for the DMU service can be seen behind the nameboard. (The Lens of Sutton Collection)

45. Here we see the down platform in the early 1960s. While mail and newspapers are being unloaded from the rear van of a down express a porter brings up items for loading. These moments of intense activity during station stops have now passed into history. (J. Osgood)

46. Pigeon traffic was once a regular feature, with the birds being released at a definite time and place to race back to their homes. Birds regain their freedom from a hamper on the down slow platform in 1960. The background is formed by a then new DMU in the up slow platform. The suffix "Midland Road' was dropped on 18th April 1966, following the closure of Bute Street the previous year. (J. Osgood)

47. Class 319 units stand in Luton station on 16th July 2002. On the right in platform No.1 is No.369 forming the 10.12 Bedford to Brighton. In platform 2 on the left is No.422 waiting to depart as the 10.46 to Sutton. (G. W. Goslin)

48. Luton's fast line platforms have been extended and can accommodate HSTs comfortably. A down HST passes on 16 July 2002. (G. W. Goslin)

49. The growth of industry in Luton eventually required the provision of additional goods facilities to supplement those of Crescent Road yard. Situated to the north, Limbury Road yard was brought into use during World War I. Limbury Road signal box, opened on 9th August 1915, controlled the connections to the goods lines. In this late 1950s view, the shunting engine, 2-6-4T No.42680, stands in front of the box while, doubtless, the crew and signalman enjoy a cup of tea. Limbury Road box was taken out of use on 9th August 1959 and replaced by a ground frame. (J. Osgood)

CG52 — MONDAYS TO FRIDAYS — Until 25 September
WIGSTON NORTH JN. TO ST. PANCRAS — UP

	2B27	6O77	5C28	2T21	6V76	1M24	2J17	6C31	6C31	6C31	6C31	2B29
	To Sevenoaks	08 33 COY Forders Sdgs to Hoo Jn. S.S.	E.C.S. to Cricklewd CS	To Brighton	08 45 COY Cliffe Hill Stud Farm to Hayes and H Tarmac S	07 34 from Leeds	To Guildford	08 31 COY Mtsorrel Sdg to Elstow Redland Sdg	08 31 COY Mtsorrel Sdg to Radlett RR	08 40 COY Humberstne Road to Elstow Redland Sdg	08 40 COY from Humberstne Road	To Sevenoaks
TIMING LOAD	EMU	D	EMU	EMU	D	HST	EMU	D	D	D	D	EMU
HEADCODE	S8		CE	H3	MX		G1	MTHO	MTHO	TWFO	TWFO	S8

		2B27	6O77	5C28	2T21	6V76	1M24	2J17	6C31	6C31	6C31	6C31	2B29
Wigston North Jn. dep	1					09 26		09 34					
Wigston South Jn.	2					GL							
Kilby Bridge Jn.	3					09*42							
Market Harborough	5					09 59		09 42					
Kettering North Junction	6					10 14			10 08	10 08	10 08	10 08	
KETTERING arr	8					10C18							
KETTERING dep	9					10*31		09 49½	10 10	10 10	10 10	10 10	
Kettering Sth Jn.	11					11*00			10 12	10 12	10 12	10 12	
Harrowden Jn.	12								10 17	10 17	10 17	10 17	
WELLINGBOROUGH arr	13								SL	SL	SL	SL	
WELLINGBOROUGH dep	14					Kilby Bridge Jn arr 09 31		09 54	10 19	10 19	10 19	10 19	
Sharnbrook Jn.	16							09 59½	10 31	10 31 [2]	10 31	10 31	
Bedford North Jn. arr	18					Kettering Nth Jn arr 10*36		10 03 ③	10*40 10*50 →	10*40 10*50 →	10*40 10*50 →	10 39 FL	
Bedford North Jn. dep	19												
BEDFORD arr	21				09 48								
BEDFORD dep	22				SL								
Bedford C.S.	23												
Bedford South Jn.	25				09 50			10 07				10 41	
Elstow arr	26												
Elstow dep	27												
Elstow Redland Sdg arr	28												
Flitwick Jn.	29				09 56½							10 58 ⓑ	
Flitwick	31				09 57½		10 11½ [1]						
Harlington	32				10 01½								
Leagrave Jn.	33				10 05½							11 11 SL [3]③	
Leagrave	35				10 06½								
Limbury Road arr	36												
LUTON arr	37				10 10		10 19½					11 21	10 30
LUTON dep	38	10 00		10*05	10 11		10 21	10 18				ⓘ	SL
Luton South Jn.	39	SL		SL				SL					10 36
Harpenden	40	10 06			10 17			10 24				11 29	10 37
Harpenden Jn.	41	10 07			10 18		10 25					ⓘ	
ST ALBANS arr	43	10 11			10 22			10 29					10 41
ST ALBANS dep	44	10 12		10 17½	10 23			10 30				11 35	10 42
Radlett Redland Roadstone arr	45			③								11 42	
Radlett	46	10 17					10 35						10 47
Radlett Jn.	47	10 18½			10 28½		10 36½						10 48½
Elstree & Borehamwood	48	10 20½	SL				10 38½					ⓘ	10 50½
Mill Hill Broadway	49	10 24½	←				10 42½					St Albans and Radlett Red. Rdstn	10 54½
Silkstream Junction	50		10 20 UHL										
Hendon	52	10 27	10 22		10 30	10 34	10 36½ [2]	10 46					10 57
Brent Curve Jn. arr	54		10*26										
Brent Curve Jn. dep	55		10*40										
Cricklewood Recess Sdg.	56												
Cricklewood C.S.	57												
Dudding Hill Jn.	58			10 45									
Cricklewood Depot Jn.	59				10 33 GL								
Cricklewood Rec Line	60												
Cricklewood U.G.L. arr	61												
Cricklewood U.G.L. dep	62												
Cricklewood Curve Jn.	63				10RMs39								
Cricklewood	64						10 49						
Cricklewood R.T.S.	65												
Cricklewood South Jn.	66												
West Hampstead Thameslink	68	10 29½			10 36½		10 40½	10 51½					10 59½
West Hampstead South Jn.	70	10 30			10 37			10 52½					11 00
Carlton Road Jn.	72	10 31½			10 38½			10 54					11 01½
Kentish Town Jn.	73												
Kentish Town	74	10 32 MOL [2]			10 39 MOL [2]		10 55 MOL [2]						11 02 MOL [2]
Kings Cross Thameslink	77	10a39½			10a46		11a02½						11a09½
Farringdon	79	10a43			10a49½		11a06						11a13
Barbican	80												
MOORGATE arr	82												
Churchyard Sidings	83												
LONDON ST PANCRAS arr	84						10 46						

Inter City, Midland and Cross Country Working Timetable 1992

LEAGRAVE

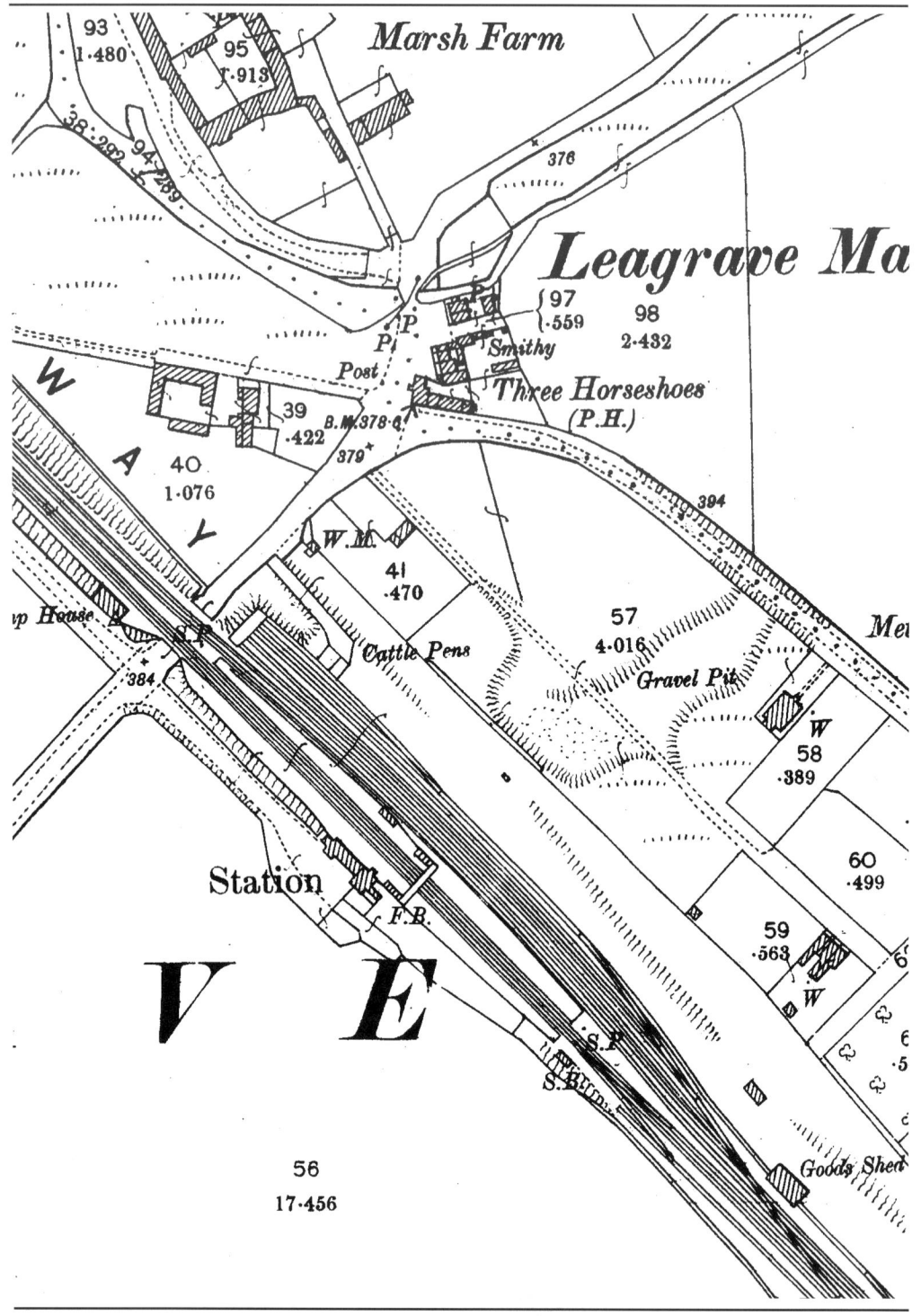

The Ordnance Survey map of 1901 shows that the surroundings of the station were then undeveloped. The marshalling sidings adjacent to the up goods line can be seen opposite the platforms.

50. Standing on the down platform in Midland Railway days, we look south before the up passenger to up goods crossover was added in 1913. At that time, a group of sidings accessed from the up goods line were used to adjust the loads of coal trains which had accomplished the main climbs and faced easier gradients onwards. The odd train was terminated and the wagons distributed in the sidings to be taken on by later trains. The engine returned to Wellingborough propelling the brake van. (G. W. Goslin collection)

51. We are still looking south, but this time the view was taken in the 1960s. An up slow platform has been added and a new footbridge to the north of the station buildings now serves all platforms in place of the original structure at the south end. (The Lens of Sutton Collection)

52. Morning light in 1960 discloses little change to the 1868 station building except the addition of lamps and signs. The motor car had not yet ousted pedal power completely and the cycle sheds were well used. (J. Osgood)

53. Class 319 No.458 departs from Leagrave's down fast platform to be turned in to the down slow line. Initially, most down electric trains used the fast line through to Bedford but with additional Midland Main Line workings the slow line is now used generally north of Harpenden or Leagrave. (G. W. Goslin)

54. A standard small shelter on the up slow platform has been surmounted by a rather ungainly roof, an architectural contrast with the building on the down-fast platform. (G. W. Goslin)

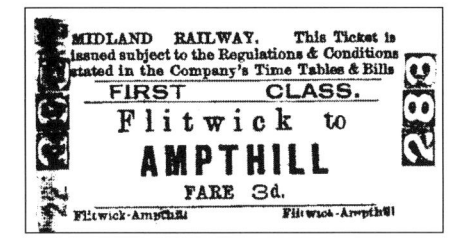

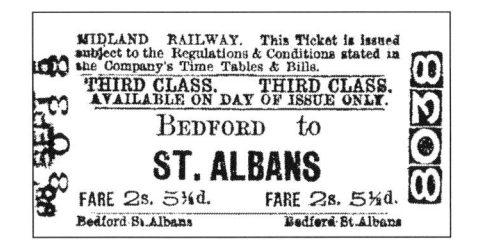

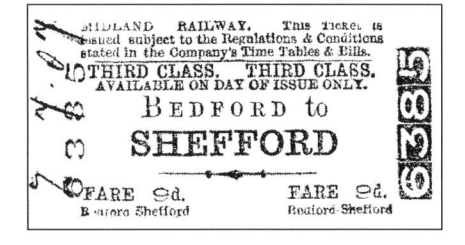

NORTH OF LEAGRAVE

55. Driver Albert Haddon takes Compound No.41048 through the high overbridge between Sundon and Leagrave with the 11.00 a.m. Bedford to St Pancras on 14th April 1952. (E. D. Bruton)

56. *Jubilee* Class 4-6-0 No.45594 *Bhopal* passes the gantry for Sundon's up home signals with the 8.40am express from Sheffield on 19th April 1952. (E. D. Bruton)

57. A well cleaned Class 5MT 4-6-0, No.45104 of Newton Heath, is on the last pitch of the climb to Milepost 33¾ with a Rugby League Cup Final excursion on 19th April 1952. (E. D. Bruton)

58. Also on the Rugby League Cup Final day, Class 5 4-6-0 No.45067, a Wakefield engine, is seen passing Sundon box with a Featherstone Rovers special from Knottingley. A forecast has been chalked on the smokebox - Rovers 17 - Barrow 10, but Barrow actually won! (E. D. Bruton)

59. Looking out from a diesel multiple unit in about 1960, we observe the steep incline from the up goods line to the cement works. Locomotives were only allowed to make the climb chimney first to ensure that the firebox crown remained covered. As a result some of the old Bedford goods engines sported tender cabs so that they could work tender first on the up pick-up goods. (J. Osgood)

BETWEEN HARLINGTON AND LEAGRAVE.

Sundon:—

Messrs. Forder & Sons Lime Works Sidings are used for stowing surplus fuel for Cement Works only. Shunting movements, other than attaching or detaching, must not be performed by L.M.S. engines at these sidings.

All traffic from Messrs. Forder & Son's cement works to be attached by L.M.S. trains must be placed by Messrs. Forder & Son in the two sidings south of the cement works, and all traffic for the cement works must be placed by L.M.S. engines on either of these two sidings as required. No shunting must be performed at the cement works for the purpose of placing wagons in position for loading or unloading, or for the purpose of sorting out wagons that are ready to be despatched.

Engines may run tender first from the up goods line as far as the second set of safety points in the line leading to Messrs. Forder's cement works for the purpose of attaching any wagons which may be standing there waiting to be attached, but no engine must run tender first beyond this point.

LMSR (Midland Division) Sectional Appendix to Working Timetable : March 1937.

HARLINGTON

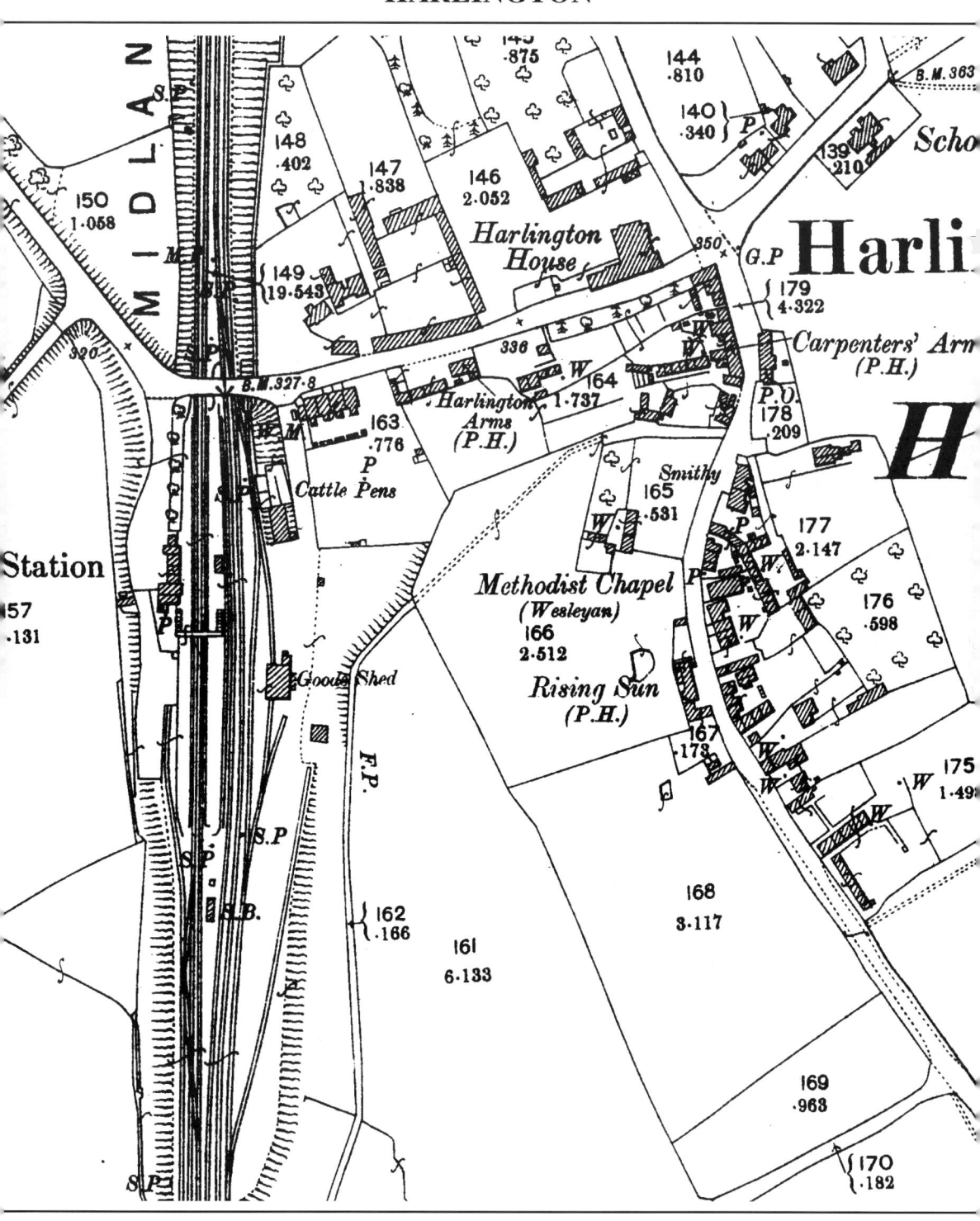

Harlington's village setting is shown on the Ordnance Survey Map of 1901. Much of its character is still retained today.

60. *Jubilee* Class 4-6-0 No. 5654 *Hood* is viewed from Harlington footbridge as she rushes through with an up express on 7th June 1939. The station was known as 'Harlington for Toddington' from 1st October 1889 until 1st November 1927. (H. C. Casserley)

61. Class 4F 0-6-0 No. 3967 stands in front of the goods shed while shunting at Harlington on 7th June 1939. The site of the goods yard is now occupied by a road transport business. (H. C. Casserley)

62. In this view we are looking north on 16th June 1951 and see the down platform with its 1913 signal box which is now preserved at the Quainton Railway Centre. The 40 lever frame faced the back of the box rather than the rails, a considerable novelty when new. (J. Osgood)

63. Looking from a train widow around 1960, we observe the down fast platform and the main building. Harlington is now the only village station on the London Extension. In 2003 it was perhaps the best preserved of the three remaining examples of the six stations which were built to the same design. (J. Osgood)

64. We stand on the footbridge in 1960, and can observe the running junction beneath the overbridge. On the right, an 8F 2-8-0 is shunting on the northern connection to the yard. The presence of this connection meant that the up slow platform was slightly staggered to the south. Although the yard has been closed for many years, this still pertains today. (J. Osgood)

65. We look south from the down fast platform in the 1960s to see the extended footbridge which served the then new up slow platform. (J. Osgood)

66. Despite the intrusion of electrical apparatus, Harlington still preserves much of its original appearance. We look from the island platform in this 2002 view. (G. W. Goslin)

67. Class 319 unit No.444 forming the 11.27 Bedford to Brighton enters the up slow platform on 16th July 2002. (G. W. Goslin)

FLITWICK

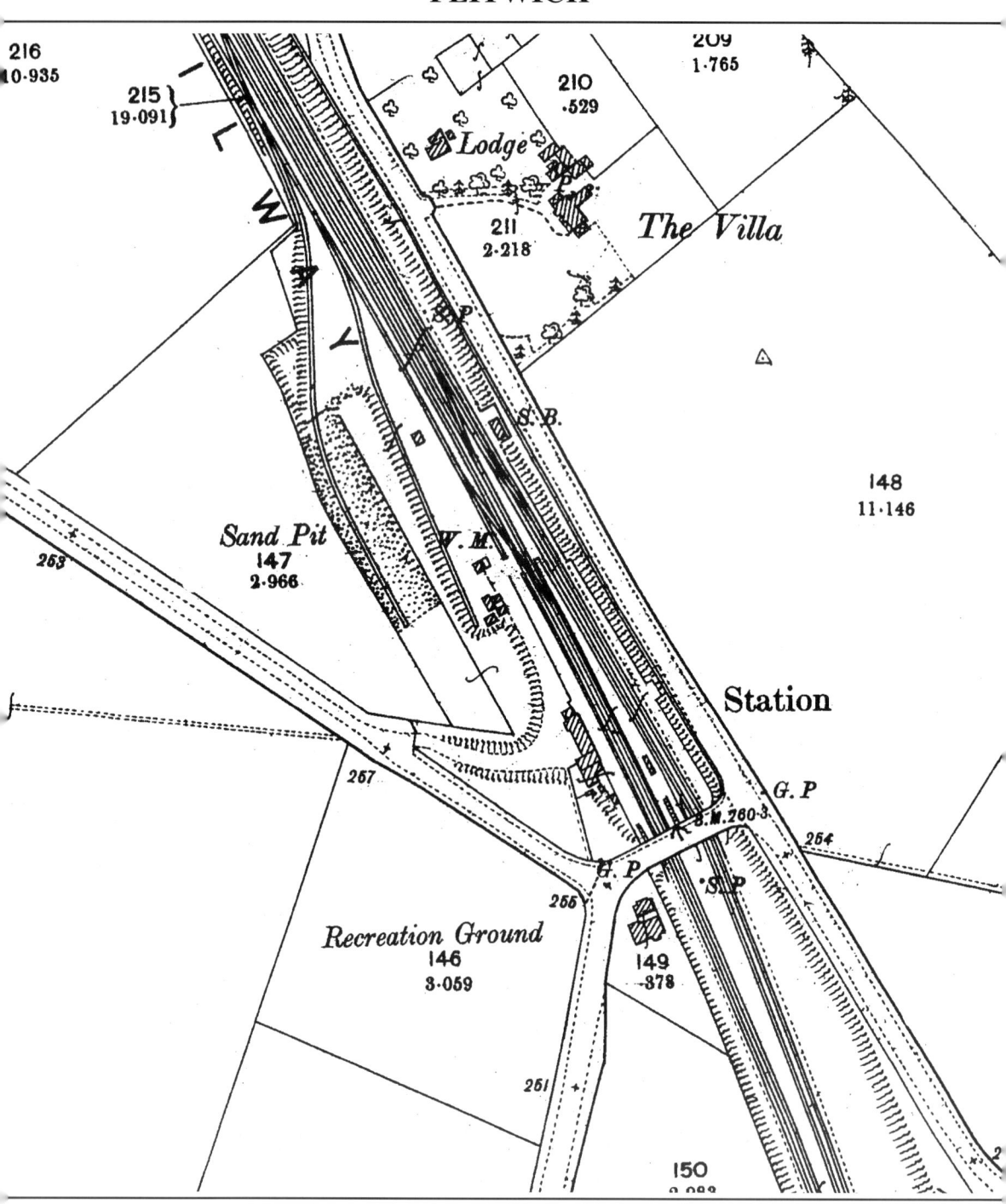

Before the line was opened to passengers, plans were being were being made for a station at Flitwick. The goods yard was originally intended to be on the east side but in the event it was unique on the Extension in being sited to the west of the main lines. The station was opened on 2nd May 1870 and is shown here on the Ordnance Survey map of 1901.

68. Passengers are waiting as Standard Class 4MT 4-6-0 No.75042 enters Flitwick with an up passenger train in the late 1950s. Bedford's shed code was 15D from 1934 but at this late stage of steam haulage it had been changed to 14E. (J. Osgood)

69. *Jubilee* Class 4-6-0 No.45636 *Uganda* runs into the station with a semi-fast from Nottingham on 14th August 1954. The ten coach train is far too long for the platform which at that time could accommodate about six coaches at the most. On the right can be seen the space available for an up slow platform and shelter made by setting back the retaining wall at the time of the widening in 1894. (J. Osgood)

70. A 4-car Rolls Royce DMU calls at the down slow platform soon after the introduction of the service in 1960. Safety considerations ensured that the decorative speed stripes soon gave way to a yellow panel and eventually to a complete yellow cab front. (J. Osgood)

71. The main building at Flitwick had totem signs and the designation of Platform 1 dates this photograph in the DMU era. But ancient parcels trolleys and steps to assist passengers using a low platform are still in evidence. (J. Osgood)

72. The 1894 Flitwick signal box is seen here on 6th June 1970. (M. A. King)

73. An engineers train with boring and concreting equipment for mast foundations is viewed on the up slow line near the signal box in September 1978. (G. W. Goslin)

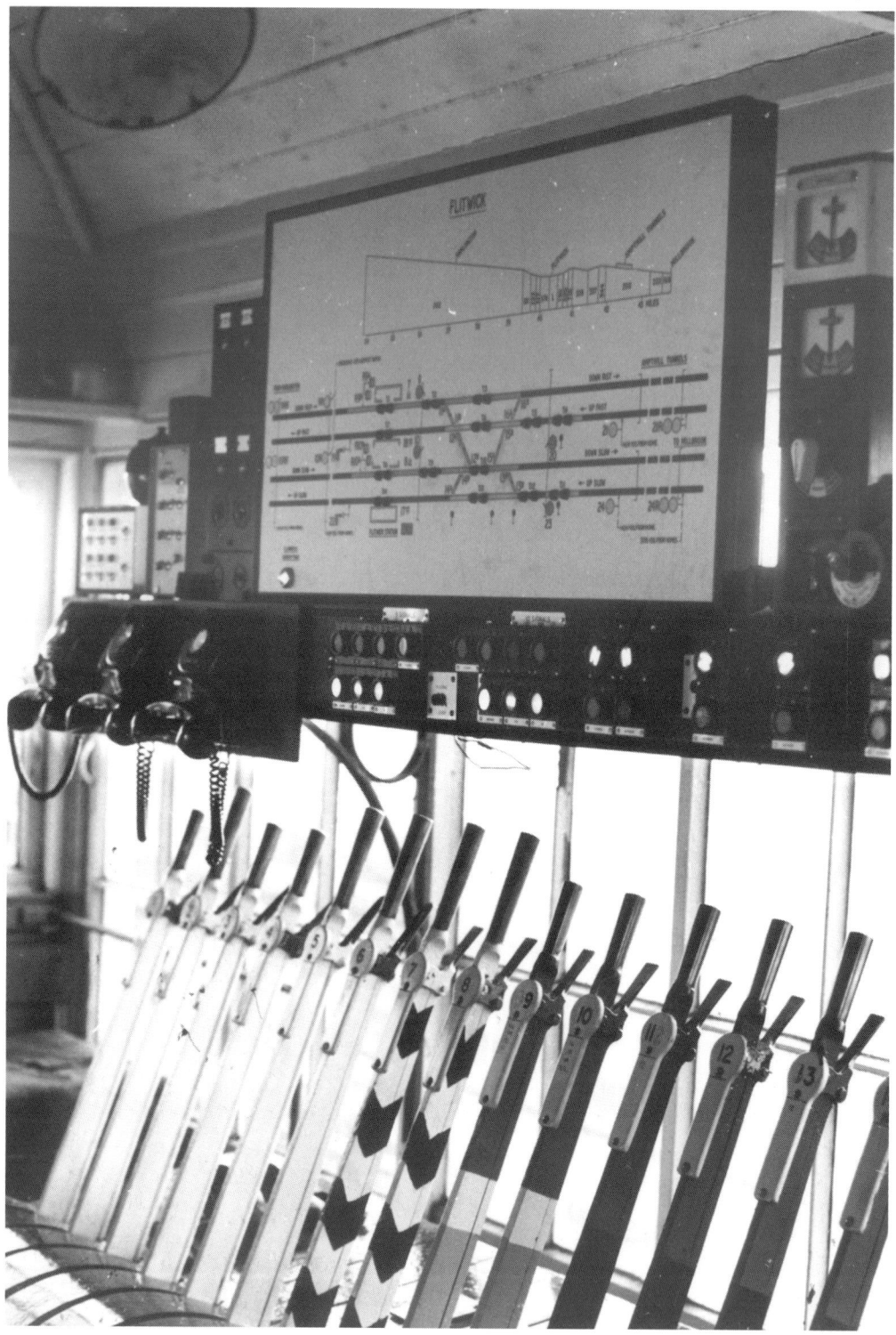

74. Here we see the signal box interior shortly before closure. The layout has already been revised for the pending electrification. It had a frame of 24 levers and was closed on 1st June 1980. (B. Cross collection)

75. Class 319 No.183 leaves Flitwick en route from Bedford to Brighton on 31st August 1995. To accommodate eight-car trains, Flitwick's platforms have been extended southwards through a rebuilt road overbridge. A further stretch for twelve cars was in prospect in 2003. (G. W. Goslin)

76. The main building in 2002 has had the one-time "gents" converted into a 24 hour taxi office. (G. W. Goslin)

AMPTHILL

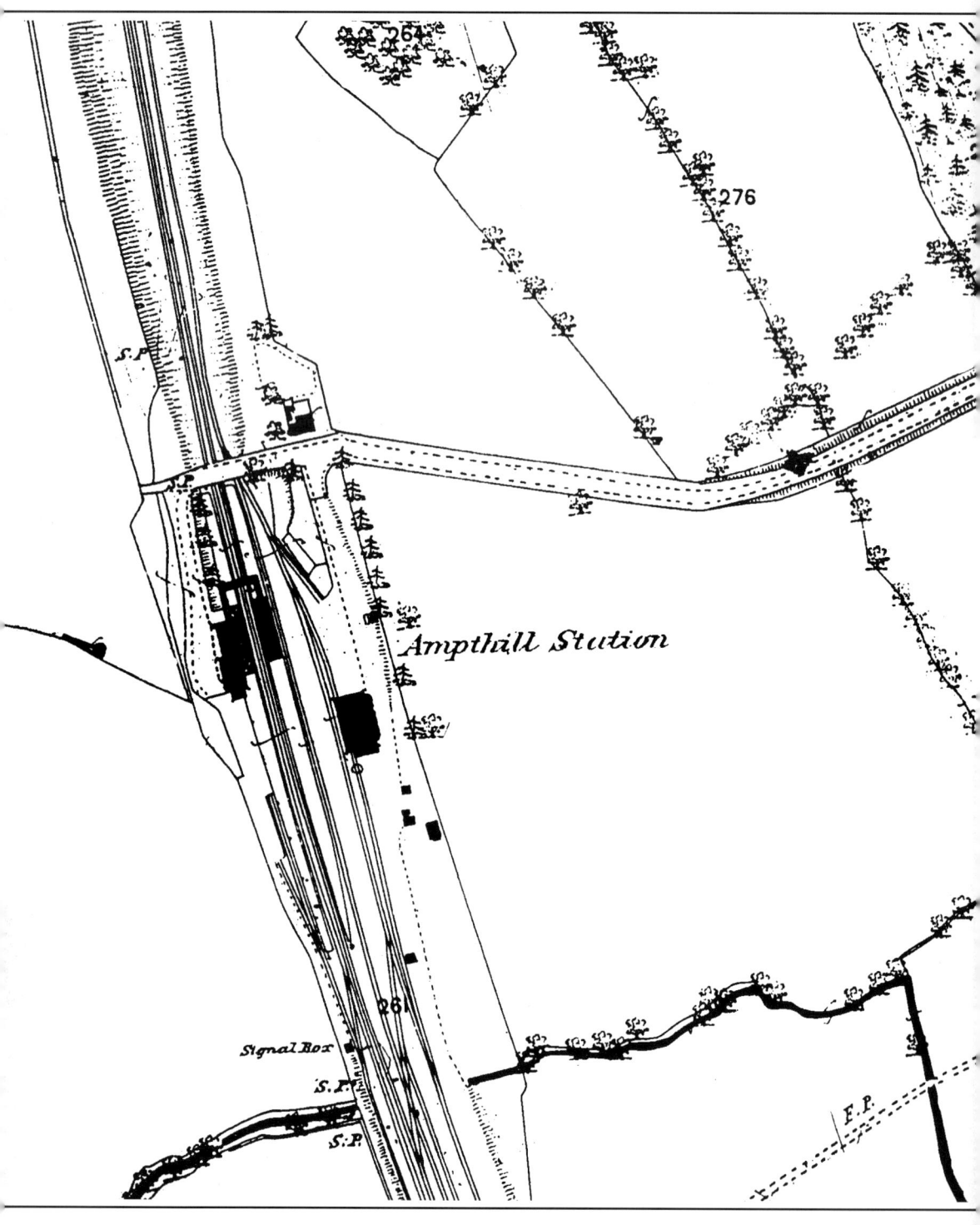

The pre-widening layout is shown in the 1882 Survey. The only habitation visible is the Station Master's house, emphasising the remoteness of the station from the town.

77. In Midland Railway days, the staff doubtless had pride in the smart appearance of Ampthill station, as we can see from this pre-1914 view of the down platform. (J. Parker collection)

78. After World War II, the station was in a run-down condition and much of its traffic had passed to nearby Flitwick. The introduction of diesel multiple unit services would have required the provision of a new up slow platform and an extension of the footbridge, but the cost could not be justified so the station closed instead. In this view, taken on the final day of opening, 3rd May 1959, tickets are collected from passengers who alighted from the penultimate down train. The last train called after dark. (J. Osgood)

79. Here we see Ampthill in May 1959, just after closure. The canopy, covered footbridge and long platforms disclose its original importance. (J. Osgood)

80. The 'stage', or ground frame at the north end is viewed with a 2F 0-6-0 on the down goods line about to set back into the yard. J. Osgood

81. An up express headed by Compound No. 41017 emerges from Ampthill tunnel into pleasant countryside about 1948. (L. N. Owen)

82. Ampthill slow lines tunnel seen from the south on 26th October 1995. This is the original bore, the later tunnel required for the quadrupling serves the fast lines in contrast to the remainder of the widening works. (G. W. Goslin)

NORTH OF AMPTHILL

83. Compound 4-4-0 No.41082 trundles along with the down afternoon milk empties between Ampthill tunnel and Millbrook box in about 1954. (G. W. Goslin)

LMSR Appendix to Working Timetable March 1937.

84. Millbrook box was opened in 1893. It was situated in an exposed position on an embankment above flat country with extensive views to the east. An anemometer was provided and when the wind speed exceeded a certain figure the single engine loads from Leicester to St Pancras were reduced. Inevitably, Millbrook became known as Windmill Junction. It had running junctions from up goods to up fast and (from 1913) down fast to down goods. After the latter addition the box had a 30 lever frame with two spares. In 1935 the up goods from Kempston Road Junction was re-designated up slow as far as Millbrook. This gave an alternative path for passenger trains from Bedford when up expresses were running late. The box was closed on 1st June 1980. (M. A. King / R. Goodman collection)

85. Roadstone has formed a large proportion of the freight traffic in recent years. No. 56103 heads an up Redland train past the site of Millbrook box on 25th April 1990. (G. W. Goslin)

86. Houghton Conquest box was situated on the up side. It was opened on 30th June 1935 to control the connections to a new brickworks, eventually known as the Coronation Works, on the opposite side of the line. It was a long box and the spare capacity gave rise to a local rumour that it was also intended as the junction of a connection to the ex-LNWR Bletchley to Cambridge line at Forders Sidings. The large volume of brick traffic on both routes at the time makes this quite likely. The closure of Houghton Conquest on 16th April 1973 left a long block section of over five miles from Millbrook to Kempston Road Junction. (M. A. King / R. Goodman collection)

87. Shunting in the sidings at the Coronation Works was performed by a four wheeled electric locomotive named *Ruth*. Power was transmitted by twin overhead lines to collectors, a system reminiscent of trolleybuses. (J. Osgood)

88. A large ordnance factory was built near the line between Houghton Conquest and Elstow boxes after the outbreak of World War II. Access to the extensive sidings was controlled by a new box, Wilshampstead, opened on 3rd August 1941. Special trains for the work force used a terminus station. A small Wilshampstead Station signal box was provided to control internal movements. It is seen here on 13th October 1969 after closure. (P. E. B. Butler)

89. The interior of Wilshamstead Station box on 13th October 1969. (P. E. B. Butler)

90. Elstow signal box in June 1939. Signalman Arthur Lunnon is at the open window. It was opened on 13th August 1893 as Elstow Junction when a up goods line from Kempston Road Junction was brought into use. The running connections with the fast lines were removed after the goods lines had been completed to the south and the box lost the title of "Junction" on 13th October 1896. It remained in use as a useful block post with control of the connection to the sidings of Elstow brickworks. Lack of run-round facilities meant that the "Elstow shunter" was a propelling movement on its return to Bedford. The box was closed on 5th November 1961. (G. W. Goslin)

91. A rare view shows the Fell diesel-mechanical locomotive No.10100 at work. It is heading an up Manchester express near Elstow box in April 1952. (D. W. F. Goslin)

SOUTH OF BEDFORD

92. This box played an important part in the operation of traffic at Bedford. It had running junctions which enabled a large proportion of the through goods and mineral trains to use the fast lines to avoid the platform lines at the station. There was also an up slow to up fast junction which provided an alternative to the junction at Bedford South for up passenger trains. (A. Vaughan)

Bedford North Junction.

Drivers approaching Bedford North Junction on the up goods line, with the signals in the "All Right" position, must not take water from the stand pipe alongside the up goods line.

Bedford Junction.

All trains leaving the Hitchin Branch, except those running on to the Hitchin platform line, must run on to the down slow line.

Between Bedford and Ampthill.

Ballast pit sidings:—

Should the movement of the bolting-lever in Kempston Road Junction Signal Box fail to release the bolt-lock on the ballast pit sidings points, the Guards must immediately communicate with the Signalman, and take his instructions as to the disposal of the train, and the Signalman must advise the Station-master at Bedford and the Telegraph Lineman for the district, in order that the necessary arrangements may be made for working the traffic and for the electrical apparatus to be put in working order.

The key of the door of the stage at the ballast pit siding is kept in Kempston Road Junction Signal Box, and Guards requiring to attach or detach vehicles in the ballast pit sidings must obtain the key from the Signalman at Kempston Road Junction. When the work at the sidings is completed, the key must be returned to the Signalman at Kempston Road Junction.

A train or engine must not enter the ballast pit sidings at night or in foggy weather unless special arrangements are made for it to do so, and a man appointed by the District Traffic Inspector is present to attend to the working.

Midland Railway Working Timetable Sectional Appendix : July 1913.

BEDFORD.

Wagons must not be loose shunted into Messrs. Allen's siding at North Junction. Wagons standing in the siding must not be moved until the guard or shunter has ascertained this can be done with safety.

Working of Passenger Trains over Up Slow Line from Kempston Road Junction to Millbrook:—

The first passenger train passing over the line after Permissive Working has been in operation will be brought to a stand at the home signal for Kempston Road Junction box, and after the signal has been taken off a green hand signal will be exhibited by the signalman which the driver must acknowledge by a short whistle, and then proceed cautiously over the line as far as Millbrook, being prepared to stop short of any obstructions.

LMSR (Midland Division) Working Timetable Sectional Appendix : March 1937.

Lines Around Bedford

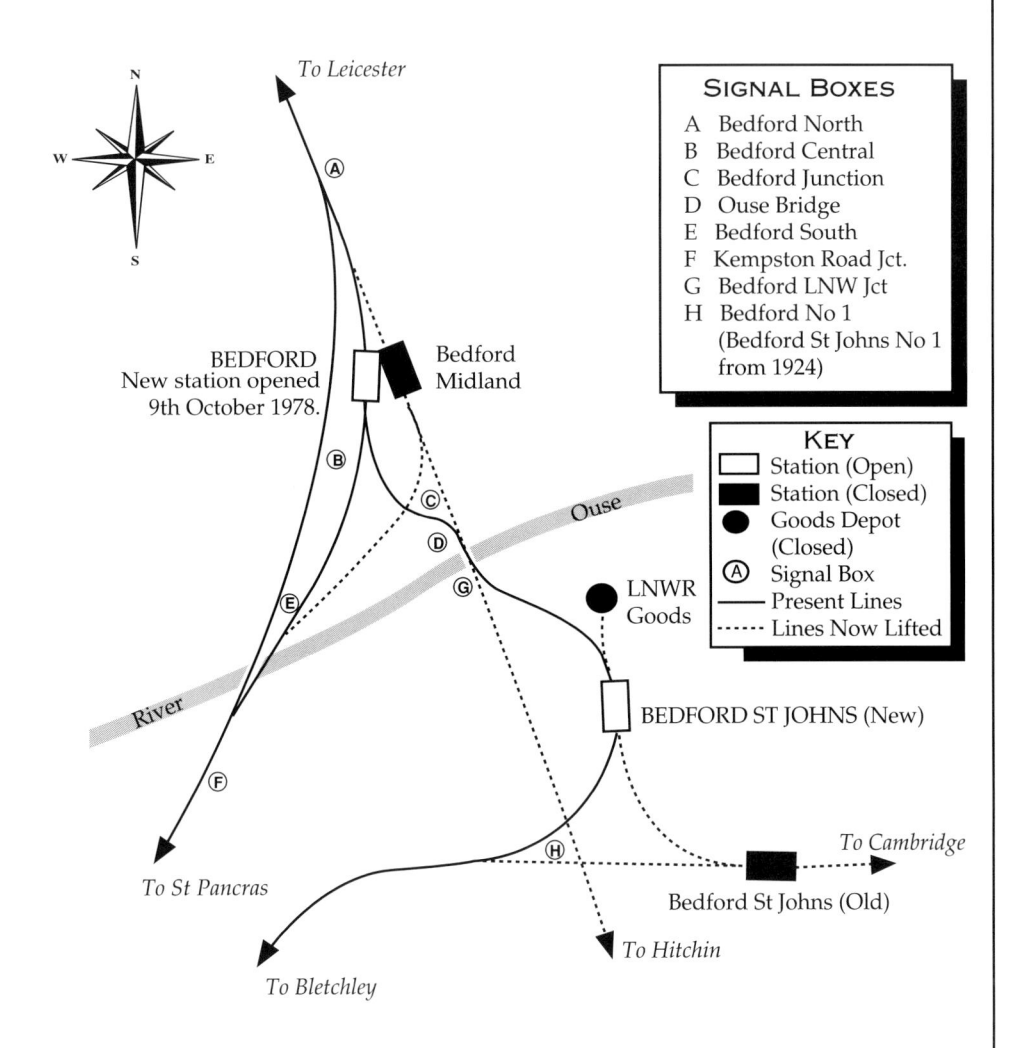

Signal Boxes
A Bedford North
B Bedford Central
C Bedford Junction
D Ouse Bridge
E Bedford South
F Kempston Road Jct.
G Bedford LNW Jct
H Bedford No 1
   (Bedford St Johns No 1 from 1924)

Key
- Station (Open)
- Station (Closed)
- Goods Depot (Closed)
- Ⓐ Signal Box
- Present Lines
- Lines Now Lifted

To Leicester

BEDFORD New station opened 9th October 1978.

Bedford Midland

Ouse

River

LNWR Goods

BEDFORD ST JOHNS (New)

To Cambridge

Bedford St Johns (Old)

To Hitchin

To St Pancras

To Bletchley

Not to scale

CDJC

93. Bedford South box was situated immediately north of the River Ouse bridges. The two pairs of lines, up and down fast and up slow and down goods, were already diverging with the fast lines curving away to avoid the station. Two standard boxes, each with its lever frame, were combined, back to back, with an interposed spacing section to bring the frontages close to the pairs of lines. An enormous roof covered the whole assembly. (G. W. Goslin collection)

94. A pre-grouping view looks north from Bedford Junction signal box. The platforms can be seen through the arch of the bridge in the foreground. The lines to St Pancras and Hitchin diverge to the left and right respectively. (The Lens of Sutton Collection)

95. On 18th November 1999 we see a Midland MainLine Class 170 Turbostar diesel multiple unit heading south from Bedford on its journey to St. Pancras. (M. Turvey)

96. 4-2-2 No.176 stands at the south end of Bedford station with an up express in about 1904. This locomotive became No.657 in the 1906 renumbering and remained in service until 1925. (National Railway Museum)

LMR Working Timetable of Passenger trains 17th June - 8th September 1963.

97. Garratt No.4998 stands in Bedford shed yard when new. Access to the shed was controlled by Bedford Central box of which this is the only known photograph. The box was closed on 2nd March 1930 after provision of an engine road to the shed from Bedford North and an additional access from Bedford South. (G. W. Goslin collection)

98. In 1934, No.1038 became the first Compound to be shedded at Bedford. She is seen outside the shed in September of that year and she remained at Bedford until withdrawal in August 1952. (A. G. Ellis)

99. 0-6-0 No.3427 is seen at rest in Bedford shed yard. A Midland crest is still carried and the photograph probably dates from the time of grouping. A "cab" has been fitted to the tender front for the long tender first duty on the up pick-up goods, necessary so that reversal up the incline at Sundon could be made chimney first. (Locomotive Publishing Company)

100. *Jubilee* 4-6-0 No. 5649, later named *Hawkins*, stands by Bedford shed on the engine road to the North box in 1935. The original shed, the "old loco", is seen in the background on the right. (G. W. Goslin collection)

101. Heading an up relief express on 29th May 1950, Hughes-Fowler Class 6P 5F 'Crab' 2-6-0 No.42855 leaves a smoke trail along the fast lines as the fireman builds up the fire for the long climb to Milepost 33¾. (G. W. Goslin)

102. On the same day, *Jubilee* Class 4-6-0 No. 45657 *Tyrwhitt* passes Bedford with an up express. (G. W. Goslin)

103. A dramatic view shows 3P 4-4-0 No.753 under the shear legs at Bedford shed. Removal of the 6ft 9ins driving wheels required the engine to be tilted to a large angle. The advent of the Garratts, which sometimes failed at Bedford with hot boxes, prompted the provision of a wheel drop in the "old loco" shed and the shear legs eventually disappeared. (G. W. Goslin collection)

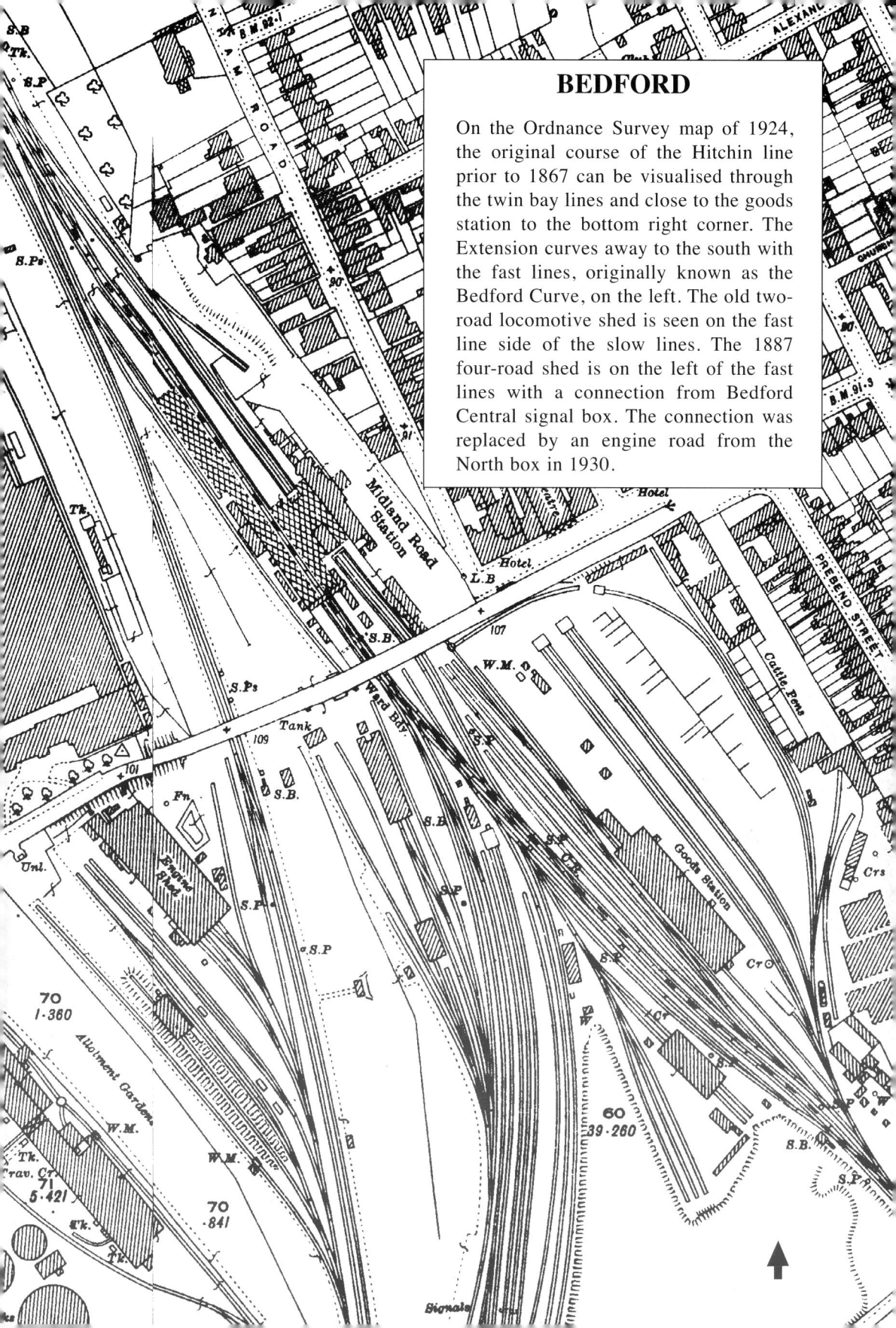

BEDFORD

On the Ordnance Survey map of 1924, the original course of the Hitchin line prior to 1867 can be visualised through the twin bay lines and close to the goods station to the bottom right corner. The Extension curves away to the south with the fast lines, originally known as the Bedford Curve, on the left. The old two-road locomotive shed is seen on the fast line side of the slow lines. The 1887 four-road shed is on the left of the fast lines with a connection from Bedford Central signal box. The connection was replaced by an engine road from the North box in 1930.

104. In this view, we look north along the original Leicester & Hitchin platforms at Bedford. When the extension to St Pancras was built these lines were cut and converted into twin bays at both the north and south ends. The refreshment room and bookstall occupied part of the space made available. (Beds County Record Office)

105. A Beyer Peacock 2-4-0 stands in the down platform at Bedford in the early days of the London Extension. Unlike the steps leading down to the platform, the footbridge itself is still uncovered. (Beds County Record Office)

106. The driver and fireman of Kirtley 800 Class 2-4-0 No. 829 pose for the camera as their locomotive stands beneath the gantry at the north end of the platforms in about 1900. (G. W. Goslin collection)

107. Here we see Bedford station in about 1914, with the grounded body of an American type Pullman Car just visible at the rear of the down platform on the left. There was a curious constriction between the platforms. The clearance between 9ft stock was only 15 inches and less between door handles. This was recognised officially. A notice for a Royal Train working to Sheffield on 23rd October 1957 stated *"BEDFORD MIDLAND ROAD - If diverted through Bedford station, the adjoining slow line must be blocked between Bedford Junction and Bedford North signal boxes."* (Locomotive & General Railway Photographs)

108. 4-2-2 No 660 has come to grief on the trap points for the siding behind the Wellingborough bay. (G. W. Goslin Collection)

109. Offices for coal merchants were provided at the entrance to the coal yard at the junction of Prebend Street and Kempston Road. They were built as part of the original Leicester & Hitchin railway. Although worthy of preservation they were destroyed in the 1960s. (G. W. Goslin collection)

110. J&F Howard's Britannia Works was situated to the west of the line to Hitchin just south of the Ouse. A producer of agricultural implements since 1859, the closure of the works in the depression of the 1930s was a major blow to Bedford. An 0-4-0T and a Grafton locomotive crane performed the internal shunting. (G. W. Goslin collection)

111. We look north from the Ouse crossing along the course of the Hitchin line towards Midland Road station on 7th July 1962. Ouse Bridge box is on the left and the goods yard and warehouse are to the right. The shunter is 3F 0-6-0T No.47485. (J. Osgood)

112. The station was renamed Bedford Midland Road on 2nd June 1924 to avoid confusion with the former LNWR station in the town which became 'Bedford St. John's' from the same date. In this view we are looking from the up platform towards the booking hall. The original up and down lines to Hitchin ran across the foreground but the platform was extended over their site when the extension was opened for passengers in 1868. (Beds County Record Office)

BEDFORD MIDLAND ROAD

WEEKDAYS

AM 1	04 MO	4	Wellingborough Midland Rd., Kettering, Market Harborough, Leicester London Rd., Trent (for Nottingham, Lincoln St. Marks), Derby Midland.
	08 MX	4	Wellingborough Midland Rd., Kettering, Market Harborough, Leicester London Rd., Derby Midland, Chesterfield Midland, Sheffield Midland, Rotherham Masboro', Cudworth, Normanton, Leeds City (for Bradford).
	23 MO	3	Luton Midland Rd., St. Albans City, Cricklewood, Kentish Town, London St. Pancras.
2	37 MO	3	Luton Midland Rd., St. Albans City, London St. Pancras.
	46 SO	3	*28th June to 6th September inclusive.* Luton Midland Rd., London St. Pancras.
3	45 MO	3	Luton Midland Rd., St. Albans City (for all stations, except Napsbury and Mill Hill Broadway, to Kentish Town), London St. Pancras.
	50 SO	3	Luton Midland Rd., St. Albans City (for all stations, except Napsbury and Mill Hill Broadway, to Kentish Town), London St. Pancras.
4	02 MSX	3	Luton Midland Rd., St. Albans City (for all stations, except Napsbury and Mill Hill Broadway, to Kentish Town), London St. Pancras.
5	12 MX	3	Luton Midland Rd., St. Albans City, London St. Pancras.
	42	4	Wellingborough Midland Rd. (for Higham Ferrers), Kettering (for Melton Mowbray), Market Harborough, Leicester London Rd. (for Nottingham, Lincoln St. Marks ; Birmingham), Loughborough Midland, Derby Midland (for Chesterfield, Sheffield, Leeds City, Bradford), Ambergate, Matlock, Miller's Dale (for Buxton), Manchester Central (for Liverpool Central).
	45 SX	3	All stations to St. Albans City (for Mill Hill Broadway, Hendon, Cricklewood, West Hampstead, Kentish Town), then Radlett, Elstree & Borehamwood, London St. Pancras.
	50 SO	3	All stations, except Napsbury, to London St. Pancras.
6	12	1	Cardington, Southill, Shefford, Henlow Camp, Hitchin.
	25 SX	3	All stations to St. Albans City, then Radlett, London St. Pancras.
	35	2	Turvey, Olney, Northampton Bridge Street, Northampton Castle (for Rugby Midland, Coventry ; also Saturdays excepted Nuneaton, Stafford, Crewe, Preston, Windermere ; Barrow, Whitehaven, Workington).
	45 SO	3	All stations to St. Albans City, then Radlett, London St. Pancras.
7	00 SX	3	All stations to Luton Midland Road.
	18 SO	3	Flitwick, Luton Midland Rd., Harpenden Central, St. Albans City, Elstree & Borehamwood, London St. Pancras.
	23 SX	3	Luton Midland Road, Harpenden Central, London St. Pancras.
	32 SO	3	All stations to St. Albans City (for all stations to West Hampstead), Kentish Town, London St. Pancras.
	32	5	Turvey, Olney, Piddington, Northampton Bridge Street, Northampton Castle (for Rugby Midland, Coventry, Birmingham; also Saturdays only Nuneaton, Stafford, Crewe, Preston, Windermere ; Barrow, Whitehaven, Workington).
	35 SX	3	All stations to St. Albans City (for all stations, except Napsbury, to Kentish Town), then London St. Pancras.
	55	3	Flitwick, Luton Midland Rd., London St. Pancras.
8	09 SX	3	All stations to St. Albans City (for all stations, except Radlett, to Kentish Town), then Radlett, London St. Pancras.
	18 SX / 23 SO	4	Oakley, Sharnbrook, Irchester, Wellingborough Midland Rd. (for Leicester, Derby, Buxton, Manchester Central, Liverpool Central).
	27 SO	3	All stations to St. Albans City (for all stations to Kentish Town), then London St. Pancras.
	43	3	Cardington, Southill, Shefford, Henlow Camp, Hitchin.
	53 SX	3	Luton Midland Road, London St. Pancras.
	54 SO	3	London St. Pancras.
9	06 SO	3	Luton Midland Rd., London St. Pancras.
	18 SX / 24 SO	4	Wellingborough Midland Rd. (for Higham Ferrers), Kettering, Market Harborough, Leicester London Rd., Loughborough Mid., Nottingham Midland (for Chesterfield, Sheffield, Leeds City, Edinburgh Waverley).
10	15 SX	3	London St. Pancras.
	23 SO	3	Luton Midland Rd. (for Harpenden, St. Albans, Radlett, Elstree & Borehamwood), London St. Pancras.
	35 SO	3	London St. Pancras.
	36 MFO	4	*9th to 27th June and 1st to 12th September inclusive.* Wellingborough Midland Rd., Kettering (for Nottingham ; Derby, Buxton, Manchester Central, Liverpool Central), Market Harborough, Leicester London Rd. (for Chesterfield, Sheffield, Leeds City, Bradford, Glasgow St. Enoch).
	36 MFO	4	*30th June to 29th August inclusive.* Wellingborough Midland Rd., Kettering (for Nottingham; Derby, Buxton, Manchester Central, Liverpool Central), Market Harborough, Leicester London Rd. (for Chesterfield, Leeds City, Bradford, Glasgow St. Enoch), Sheffield Midland.
	36 TWThO	4	Wellingborough Midland Rd., Kettering (for Nottingham ; Derby, Buxton, Manchester Central, Liverpool Central), Market Harborough, Leicester London Rd. (for Chesterfield, Sheffield, Leeds City, Bradford, Glasgow St. Enoch).
	38 SO	4	*14th and 21st June only.* Wellingborough Midland Rd. (for Higham Ferrers), Kettering (for Derby, Buxton, Manchester Central, Liverpool Central), Market Harborough, Leicester London Rd. (for Nottingham ; Chesterfield, Sheffield, Leeds City, Bradford, Glasgow St. Enoch).
	38 SO	4	*28th June to 30th August inclusive.* Wellingborough Midland Rd. (for Higham Ferrers), Kettering (for Derby, Buxton, Manchester Central, Liverpool Central), Market Harborough, Leicester London Rd. (for Nottingham; Chesterfield, Leeds City, Bradford), Sheffield Midland, Carlisle, Annan, Dumfries, Kilmarnock, Glasgow St. Enoch. Buffet Car.
	38 SO	4	*6th and 13th September only.* Wellingborough Midland Rd. (for Higham Ferrers), Kettering (for Derby, Buxton, Manchester Central, Liverpool Central), Market Harborough, Leicester London Rd. (for Nottingham ; Chesterfield, Leeds City, Bradford, Glasgow St. Enoch), Sheffield Midland.
	52 SO	3	All stations, except Napsbury, to London St. Pancras.
11	00 SX	3	All stations, except Napsbury, to London St. Pancras.
	10 SO	5	Turvey, Olney, Piddington, Northampton Bridge Street, Northampton Castle (for Rugby Midland, Coventry, Birmingham).
	28 SX	3	Luton Midland Rd., Harpenden Central, St. Albans City (for all stations to Kentish Town), London St. Pancras.
	51	3	Luton Midland Road, London St. Pancras. Restaurant Car.
PM 12	12 SO	3	Luton Midland Rd., Harpenden Central, St. Albans City (for all stations, except Napsbury, to Kentish Town), then London St. Pancras.
	30 SX	4	Wellingborough Midland Rd. (for Higham Ferrers), Kettering (for Melton Mowbray ; Nottingham, Lincoln St. Marks ; Derby, Buxton, Manchester Central, Liverpool Central ; Sheffield, Leeds City, Bradford), Desborough & Rothwell, Market Harborough, Kibworth, Leicester London Rd.
	32 SO	4	Wellingborough Midland Rd. (for Higham Ferrers), Kettering (for Nottingham, Lincoln St. Marks ; Derby, Buxton, Manchester Central, Liverpool Central, Sheffield, Leeds City, Bradford), Market Harborough, Leicester London Rd.
	32 SO	3	All stations to Luton Midland Road.
	40 SO	5	Turvey, Olney, Piddington, Northampton Bridge Street, Northampton Castle (for Rugby Midland, Coventry, Birmingham ; Nuneaton, Stafford, Crewe).
1	20 SO	3	Luton Midland Rd., Harpenden Central, St. Albans City, Elstree & Borehamwood, London St. Pancras.
	30 SX	2	Turvey, Olney, Piddington, Northampton Bridge Street, Northampton Castle (for Rugby Midland).
	35 SX	3	All stations to St. Albans City, then Radlett, Elstree & Borehamwood, London St. Pancras.
	40 SO	2	Turvey, Olney, Piddington, Northampton Bridge Street, Northampton Castle (for Rugby Midland).
	55 SX	1	Cardington, Southill, Shefford, Henlow Camp, Hitchin.
	55 SO	3	All stations, except Napsbury, to London St. Pancras.
2	05 SX	4	Wellingborough Midland Road, Kettering (for Melton Mowbray, Nottingham, Lincoln St. Marks ; Chesterfield, Sheffield, Leeds City, Bradford), Market Harborough, Leicester London Rd. (for Derby, Buxton, Manchester Central, Liverpool Central).
	10 SO	1	Cardington, Southill, Shefford, Henlow Camp, Hitchin.
	16 SX	3	Luton Midland Rd. (for all stations, except Napsbury, to Kentish Town), London St. Pancras.
	20 SO	4	Oakley, Sharnbrook, Irchester, Wellingborough Midland Rd. (for Higham Ferrers), Kettering, Oakham, Melton Mowbray, Nottingham Midland (for Lincoln St. Marks ; Chesterfield, Sheffield, Leeds City, Bradford).
	26 SO	3	Luton Midland Road, London St. Pancras.
	50 SO	3	Luton Midland Rd., Harpenden Central, St. Albans City, Radlett, Elstree & Borehamwood, Mill Hill Broadway, London St. Pancras.
3	05 SX	3	Luton Midland Rd., Harpenden Central, St. Albans City, Radlett, Elstree & Borehamwood, Mill Hill Broadway, London St. Pancras.
	42 SX	4	Wellingborough Midland Rd., Kettering (for Nottingham, Mansfield, Lincoln St. Marks ; Chesterfield, Sheffield, Leeds City, Bradford), Market Harborough, Leicester London Rd. (for Loughborough).
4	12 SX	3	London St. Pancras. Restaurant Car.
	20 SX	3	Flitwick, Harlington, Luton Midland Rd., Harpenden Central, St. Albans City (for Mill Hill Broadway, Hendon, Cricklewood, Kentish Town), Radlett, Elstree & Borehamwood, West Hampstead Midland, London St. Pancras.
	27 SO	3	Luton Midland Road, London St. Pancras. Restaurant Car.
	36 SX	4	Oakley, Sharnbrook, Irchester, Wellingborough Midland Rd., Kettering (for Nottingham ; Leicester, Derby, Buxton, Manchester Central, Liverpool Central ; Chesterfield, Sheffield, Leeds City, Bradford).
	40 SO	3	Flitwick, Harlington, Luton Midland Rd., Harpenden Central, St. Albans City (for all stations, except Napsbury and Elstree & Borehamwood, to Kentish Town), Elstree & Borehamwood, London St. Pancras.
	41 SO	4	Oakley, Sharnbrook, Irchester, Wellingborough Midland Rd., (for Higham Ferrers), Kettering (for Leicester London Rd., Derby, Buxton, Manchester Central, Liverpool Central ; Chesterfield, Sheffield, Leeds City, Bradford).
	44 SX / 45 SO	5	Turvey, Olney, Northampton Bridge Street, Northampton Castle (for Rugby Midland, Coventry ; Birmingham, Wolverhampton).
	[illegible] SX	3	London St. Pancras.
5	[illegible] SO	3	London St. Pancras.
	25 SX	3	All stations, except Napsbury, to London St. Pancras.
	[illegible] SO	3	All stations, except Napsbury, to London St. Pancras.
	[illegible] SX	3	Luton Midland Road, Harpenden Central, St. Albans City, London St. Pancras.
	[illegible] SO	1	Cardington, Southill, Shefford, Henlow Camp, Hitchin.
	53 SX	1	Cardington, Southill, Shefford, Henlow Camp, Hitchin.
6	[illegible] SX	4	Wellingborough Midland Rd. (for Higham Ferrers), Kettering (for Leicester), Nottingham Midland (for Lincoln St. Marks). Restaurant Car.
	05 SO	4	Wellingborough Midland Rd. (for Higham Ferrers), Kettering (for Leicester), Corby, Manton, Oakham, Melton Mowbray, Nottingham Midland (for Lincoln St. Marks).
	12 SX / 17 SO	2	Oakley, Sharnbrook, Irchester, Wellingborough Midland Rd., Kettering.
	30 FSX	3	Flitwick, Luton Midland Road, Harpenden Central, St. Albans City, London St. Pancras.
	31 SO	3	Luton Midland Road, Harpenden Central, St. Albans City, London St. Pancras.
	35 FO	3	Flitwick, Luton Midland Road, Harpenden Central, St. Albans City, London St. Pancras.
	41 SX / 42 SO	4	Wellingborough Midland Rd. (for Higham Ferrers, Northampton SX), Kettering (for Melton Mowbray, Nottingham ; Derby), Market Harborough, Leicester London Road.
	46 SO	3	All stations, except Napsbury, to London St. Pancras.
7	30 FSX / 35 FO	3	All stations, except Napsbury, to London St. Pancras.
	51	4	Leicester London Rd. (for Birmingham ; Nottingham, Lincoln St. Marks), Loughborough Midland, Derby Midland (for Chesterfield, Sheffield), Matlock, Miller's Dale (for Buxton), Chinley, Didsbury, Manchester Central.
8	25	4	Wellingborough Midland Rd. (for Higham Ferrers), Kettering, Desborough & Rothwell, Market Harborough, Leicester London Road (for Loughborough, Nottingham).
	27 SX	3	Flitwick, Luton Midland Rd., Harpenden Central, St. Albans City (for all stations, except Napsbury, to Kentish Town), London St. Pancras.
	30	5	Turvey, Olney, Northampton Bridge Street, Northampton Castle.
	36 SO	3	Flitwick, Luton Midland Rd., Harpenden Central, St. Albans City (for all stations, except Napsbury, to Kentish Town), London St. Pancras.
9	17 FO	4	*27th June to 1st August inclusive.* Kettering, Leicester London Road, Loughborough Midland, Derby Midland, Leeds City, Carlisle, Dumfries, Kilmarnock, Glasgow St. Enoch.
	30	4	Wellingborough Midland Rd. (for Northampton; Higham Ferrers; Chesterfield, Bradford, Glasgow), Kettering (for Nottingham, Sheffield, Leeds City, Edinburgh Waverley), Market Harborough, Leicester London Rd., Derby Midland (for York, Newcastle).
	50	3	Luton Midland Rd., London St. Pancras.
10	10 SX	3	All stations, except Napsbury and West Hampstead Midland, to London St. Pancras.
	10 SO	3	All stations, except Napsbury and West Hampstead Midland, to London St. Pancras.

Weekday departures from Bedford Midland Road : 9th June - 14th September 1958.

113. The exterior of the station is seen in September 1978, a month before closure. At that time work was in progress on the track and platforms for the changeover to the new station. The exterior, however, still remained untouched, although the nameboard shows no sign of the suffix 'Midland Road', as the official title had been amended to 'Bedford Midland' on 8th May 1978. The site is now occupied by a DIY store. (G. W. Goslin)

114. The new station was built somewhat to the north on a revised alignment alongside the fast lines. Formal opening took place on 9th October 1978 although final completion of the works was not achieved until 1980. It initially carried the name Bedford Midland, but the suffix was dropped from 5th May 1988. Here we see the remains of the old up platform in September 1980. The new platforms can be seen on the far left. The parcels van on the right is on a bay line which was temporarily reinstated. (G. W. Goslin)

115. As part of the electrification programme, berthing sidings for electric multiple units were laid down on what was previously waste ground. 319 unit No.003 in Network SouthEast livery is seen on 25th April 1990. (G. W. Goslin)

116. In this photograph, taken on 25th April 1990, we are looking from the same position as picture 111. A signal post marks the site of Ouse Bridge box and the single line, which now proceeds from Bletchley rather than Hitchin, takes a broad sweep to the site of the new station. The EMU berthing sidings are on the left. (G. W. Goslin)

117. Engineering work on the West Coast line in 1991 required the diversion of Liverpool services to St Pancras via Nuneaton and Wigston. The trains, including their electric locomotives, were diesel hauled between Nuneaton and Bedford. Electric power resumed between Bedford and St Pancras. 87021 *Robert the Bruce* is about to leave Platform No.1 at Bedford with the 09.10 ex Liverpool on 12th October 1991. (G. W. Goslin)

118. Standing on Platform 2, we see Class 319 unit No.169 which was about to form the 12.48 to Brighton on 12th October 1991. (G. W. Goslin)

119. Red liveried EW&S No.58016 stands in the yard on 12th October 1996. The shed on the left is used to house maintenance vehicles. The building is of generally recent construction. However, the wall nearer the locomotive incorporates the side arches of Bedford's original locomotive shed (the "old loco") of 1868 which was superseded as long ago as 1887 by the "new loco", situated to the west of the fast lines. (P. G. Barnes)

120. Additional Midland Main Line services required the provision of a new platform on the down fast line. It is seen under construction on 26th May 1999 together with the footbridge extension. Bedford now has its best train service of all time. (G. W. Goslin)

MP Middleton Press

Easebourne Lane, Midhurst, W Sussex. GU29 9AZ Tel: 01730 813169 Fax: 01730 812601
Email: enquiries@middletonpress.fsnet.co.uk *If books are not available from your local transport stockist, order direct with cheque, Visa or Mastercard, post free UK.*

BRANCH LINES
Branch Line to Allhallows
Branch Line to Alton
Branch Lines around Ascot
Branch Line to Ashburton
Branch Lines around Bodmin
Branch Line to Bude
Branch Lines around Canterbury
Branch Lines around Chard & Yeovil
Branch Line to Cheddar
Branch Lines around Cromer
Branch Line to the Derwent Valley
Branch Lines to East Grinstead
Branch Lines of East London
Branch Lines to Effingham Junction
Branch Lines around Exmouth
Branch Lines to Falmouth, Helston & St. Ives
Branch Line to Fairford
Branch Lines around Gosport
Branch Line to Hayling
Branch Lines to Henley, Windsor & Marlow
Branch Line to Hawkhurst
Branch Line to Ilfracombe
Branch Line to Kingsbridge
Branch Line to Kingswear
Branch Line to Lambourn
Branch Lines to Launceston & Princetown
Branch Lines to Longmoor
Branch Line to Looe
Branch Line to Lyme Regis
Branch Line to Lynton
Branch Lines around March
Branch Lines around Midhurst
Branch Line to Minehead
Branch Line to Moretonhampstead
Branch Lines to Newport (IOW)
Branch Lines to Newquay
Branch Lines around North Woolwich
Branch Line to Padstow
Branch Lines around Plymouth
Branch Lines to Princes Risborough
Branch Lines to Seaton and Sidmouth
Branch Lines around Sheerness
Branch Line to Shrewsbury
Branch Line to Swanage *updated*
Branch Line to Tenterden
Branch Lines around Tiverton
Branch Lines to Torrington
Branch Lines to Tunbridge Wells
Branch Line to Upwell
Branch Lines of West London
Branch Lines of West Wiltshire
Branch Lines around Weymouth
Branch Lines around Wimborne
Branch Lines around Wisbech

NARROW GAUGE
Branch Line to Lynton
Branch Lines around Portmadoc 1923-46
Branch Lines around Porthmadog 1954-94
Branch Line to Southwold
Douglas to Port Erin
Douglas to Peel
Kent Narrow Gauge
Northern France Narrow Gauge
Romneyrail
Southern France Narrow Gauge
Sussex Narrow Gauge
Surrey Narrow Gauge
Swiss Narrow Gauge
Two-Foot Gauge Survivors
Vivarais Narrow Gauge

SOUTH COAST RAILWAYS
Ashford to Dover
Bournemouth to Weymouth
Brighton to Worthing
Eastbourne to Hastings
Hastings to Ashford
Portsmouth to Southampton
Ryde to Ventnor
Southampton to Bournemouth

SOUTHERN MAIN LINES
Basingstoke to Salisbury
Bromley South to Rochester
Crawley to Littlehampton
Dartford to Sittingbourne
East Croydon to Three Bridges
Epsom to Horsham
Exeter to Barnstaple
Exeter to Tavistock
Faversham to Dover
London Bridge to East Croydon
Orpington to Tonbridge
Tonbridge to Hastings
Salisbury to Yeovil
Sittingbourne to Ramsgate
Swanley to Ashford
Tavistock to Plymouth
Three Bridges to Brighton
Victoria to Bromley South
Victoria to East Croydon
Waterloo to Windsor
Waterloo to Woking
Woking to Portsmouth
Woking to Southampton
Yeovil to Exeter

EASTERN MAIN LINES
Barking to Southend
Ely to Kings Lynn
Ely to Norwich
Fenchurch Street to Barking
Hitchin to Peterborough
Ilford to Shenfield
Ipswich to Saxmundham
Liverpool Street to Ilford
Saxmundham to Yarmouth
Tilbury Loop

WESTERN MAIN LINES
Bristol to Taunton
Didcot to Banbury
Didcot to Swindon
Ealing to Slough
Exeter to Newton Abbot
Newton Abbot to Plymouth
Newbury to Westbury
Paddington to Ealing
Paddington to Princes Risborough
Plymouth to St. Austell
Princes Risborough to Banbury
Reading to Didcot
Slough to Newbury
St. Austell to Penzance
Swindon to Bristol
Taunton to Exeter
Westbury to Taunton

MIDLAND MAIN LINES
St. Albans to Bedford
Euston to Harrow & Wealdstone
St. Pancras to St. Albans

COUNTRY RAILWAY ROUTES
Abergavenny to Merthyr
Andover to Southampton
Bath to Evercreech Junction
Bath Green Park to Bristol
Burnham to Evercreech Junction
Cheltenham to Andover
Croydon to East Grinstead
Didcot to Winchester
East Kent Light Railway
Fareham to Salisbury
Frome to Bristol
Guildford to Redhill
Reading to Basingstoke
Reading to Guildford
Redhill to Ashford
Salisbury to Westbury
Stratford upon Avon to Cheltenham
Strood to Paddock Wood
Taunton to Barnstaple
Wenford Bridge to Fowey
Westbury to Bath
Woking to Alton
Yeovil to Dorchester

GREAT RAILWAY ERAS
Ashford from Steam to Eurostar
Clapham Junction 50 years of change
Festiniog in the Fifties
Festiniog in the Sixties
Festiniog 50 years of enterprise
Isle of Wight Lines 50 years of change
Railways to Victory 1944-46
Return to Blaenau 1970-82
SECR Centenary album
Talyllyn 50 years of change
Wareham to Swanage 50 years of change
Yeovil 50 years of change

LONDON SUBURBAN RAILWAYS
Caterham and Tattenham Corner
Charing Cross to Dartford
Clapham Jn. to Beckenham Jn.
Crystal Palace (HL) & Catford Loop
East London Line
Finsbury Park to Alexandra Palace
Holbourn Viaduct to Lewisham
Kingston and Hounslow Loops
Lewisham to Dartford
Lines around Wimbledon
Liverpool Street to Chingford
London Bridge to Addiscombe
Mitcham Junction Lines
North London Line
South London Line
West Croydon to Epsom
West London Line
Willesden Junction to Richmond
Wimbledon to Beckenham
Wimbledon to Epsom

STEAMING THROUGH
Steaming through Cornwall
Steaming through the Isle of Wight
Steaming through Kent
Steaming through West Hants

TRAMWAY CLASSICS
Aldgate & Stepney Tramways
Barnet & Finchley Tramways
Bath Tramways
Brighton's Tramways
Bristol's Tramways
Burton & Ashby Tramways
Camberwell & W.Norwood Tramways
Clapham & Streatham Tramways
Croydon's Tramways
Dover's Tramways
East Ham & West Ham Tramways
Edgware and Willesden Tramways
Eltham & Woolwich Tramways
Embankment & Waterloo Tramways
Exeter & Taunton Tramways
Fulwell - Home to Trams, Trolleys and Buses
Great Yarmouth Tramways
Greenwich & Dartford Tramways
Hammersmith & Hounslow Tramways
Hampstead & Highgate Tramways
Hastings Tramways
Holborn & Finsbury Tramways
Ilford & Barking Tramways
Kingston & Wimbledon Tramways
Lewisham & Catford Tramways
Liverpool Tramways 1. Eastern Routes
Liverpool Tramways 2. Southern Routes
Liverpool Tramways 3. Northern Routes
Maidstone & Chatham Tramways
Margate to Ramsgate
North Kent Tramways
Norwich Tramways
Reading Tramways
Seaton & Eastbourne Tramways
Shepherds Bush & Uxbridge Tramways
Southend-on-sea Tramways
South London Line Tramways 1903-33
Southwark & Deptford Tramways
Stamford Hill Tramways
Twickenham & Kingston Tramways
Victoria & Lambeth Tramways
Waltham Cross & Edmonton Tramways
Walthamstow & Leyton Tramways
Wandsworth & Battersea Tramways

TROLLEYBUS CLASSICS
Croydon Trolleybuses
Derby Trolleybuses
Hastings Trolleybuses
Huddersfield Trolleybuses
Maidstone Trolleybuses
Portsmouth Trolleybuses
Reading Trolleybuses
Woolwich & Dartford Trolleybuses

WATERWAY ALBUMS
Kent and East Sussex Waterways
London to Portsmouth Waterway
West Sussex Waterways

MILITARY BOOKS
Battle over Portsmouth
Battle over Sussex 1940
Blitz over Sussex 1941-42
Bombers over Sussex 1943-45
Bognor at War
Military Defence of West Sussex
Military Signals from the South Coast
Secret Sussex Resistance
Surrey Home Guard

OTHER RAILWAY BOOKS
Index to all Middleton Press stations
Industrial Railways of the South-East
South Eastern & Chatham Railways
London Chatham & Dover Railway
London Termini - Past and Proposed
War on the Line (SR 1939-45)

BIOGRAPHY
Garraway Father & Son